D1554134

Lynda Manson's professional activities include teaching, textile and clothing design, restauranteur, author of two published cookbooks, and fine arts painter.

Marcel Croteau, a native of Northern Alberta and a WWII Canadian veteran of RAF Bomber Command, was decorated by King George VI with the Distinguished Flying Medal and received many other medals for his service, including the French Knight of the Legion of Honour Medal. After the war, Marcel resumed life as a civilian, becoming a husband, father, entrepreneur, property developer, and factory owner. He is also an artist and storyteller. Marcel celebrated his 96th birthday on April 6, 2019.

This book is dedicated to Marcel's children: Edouard, George, Guy, Brian, and Christine and everyone who has suffered from the consequences of war.

Lynda Manson and
Marcel Croteau

CONQUERING THE
WAR WITHIN

Conversations with a WWII RCAF Rear Air Gunner

AUSTIN MACAULEY PUBLISHERS™

LONDON • CAMBRIDGE • NEW YORK • SHARJAH

Ordering Information:
Quantity sales: special discounts are available on quantity purchases by corporations, associations, and others. For details, contact the publisher at the address below.

Publisher's Cataloging-in-Publication data
Manson, Lynda and Croteau, Marcel
Conquering the War Within
Conversations with a WWII RCAF Rear Air Gunner

ISBN 9781643787077 (Paperback)
ISBN 9781643787060 (Hardback)
ISBN 9781645364924 (ePub e-book)

The main category of the book — History / Military / World War II

www.austinmacauley.com/us

First Published (2019)
Austin Macauley Publishers LLC
40 Wall Street, 28th Floor
New York, NY 10005
USA

mail-usa@austinmacauley.com
+1 (646) 5125767

I owe a huge debt of gratitude to Marcel Croteau for sharing the details of his life as a son, a brother, a husband, a father, a grandfather, and great grandfather. Without his willingness to reveal his experiences and struggles as a WWII Veteran and as a civilian, this book would never have happened. This is Marcel's story and his alone.

I am also very thankful to family; including James, Dave, Michael, and Cheryl, who encouraged me to undertake this project and offered valuable critiques. A huge thanks to friends who helped edit the manuscript: Judy, Dave, and Marilyn. I especially want to thank my husband Hal who provided his editing skills and unwavering support and suggestions throughout the writing of this book.

A special thanks to J. P. Cormier for allowing lyrics from his song *Hometown Battle* to be used.

Any errors or omissions are all mine.

Lynda Manson

Hometown Battleground

He got home from the service as the spring began its turn,
Twelve long months away
He folded up his uniform with the medals tucked inside
Started living for today

But the present could not find him, nor could his wife and kids
He was there but he was gone
And soon his only comfort was a bottle and his gun
Something right that went so wrong

And the silence keeps on coming as the movie plays again
He can smell the yellow dust and death hanging in the wind
And we thought the war was over, but the headlines do reveal
That another soldier died on the hometown battlefield

From the song *Hometown Battleground* by Canadian singer / songwriter J. P. Cormier

The Prose of My Life

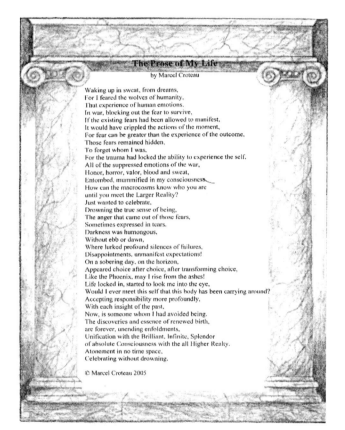

The Prose of My Life

by Marcel Croteau

Waking up in sweat, from dreams,
For I feared the wolves of humanity,
That experience of human emotions.
In war, blocking out the fear to survive,
If the existing fears had been allowed to manifest,
It would have crippled the actions of the moment,
For fear can be greater than the experience of the outcome.
Those fears remained hidden.
To forget whom I was,
For the trauma had locked the ability to experience the self.
All of the suppressed emotions of the war,
Honor, horror, valor, blood and sweat,
Entombed, mummified in my consciousness.
How can the macrocosms know who you are
until you meet the Larger Reality?
Just wanted to celebrate,
Drowning the true sense of being,
The anger that came out of those fears,
Sometimes expressed in tears.
Darkness was humongous,
Without ebb or dawn,
Where lurked profound silences of failures,
Disappointments, unmanifest expectations!
On a sobering day, on the horizon,
Appeared choice after choice, after transforming choice,
Like the Phoenix, may I rise from the ashes!
Life locked in, started to look me into the eye,
Would I ever meet this self that this body has been carrying around?
Accepting responsibility more profoundly,
With each insight of the past,
Now, is someone whom I had avoided being.
The discoveries and essence of renewed birth,
are forever, unending enfoldments,
Unification with the Brilliant, Infinite, Splendor
of absolute Consciousness with the all Higher Realty.
Atonement in no time space,
Celebrating without drowning.

Illustrations

Chapter 1

'Since there is nothing
so well worth having as friends,
never lose a chance to make them.'
– Francisco Guicciardini

Ours was a chance encounter. It was an ordinary day, neither hot nor cold, neither sunny nor overcast, devoid of expectations and plans for the future. My day was to be spent in a local co-operative art gallery where I was a member. I looked forward to meeting and greeting art lovers and collectors who I hoped would leave the gallery with smiles on their faces and a purchase in their hands. The morning had been quiet until a pleasant looking (most would say handsome), well-dressed man with a book in his hand walked through the door.

He was tall with dark hair and an engaging smile. As we greeted each other and introduced ourselves as Lynda and Marcel, he spoke with a soft and gentle French Canadian accent. He told me the purpose of his visit was to return a book he borrowed from one of the artists. We casually walked among the displays of artwork by various local artists until we came to a painting of a Wellington bomber from WWII. Marcel stopped to admire the realistic image in front of us and then turned to look at me while he told me he had briefly trained in a Wellington bomber during the war. I hoped the surprise of his revelation was not written all over my face but I could not believe this man could be old enough to have participated in a war that took place so long ago. After all, that would make him as old as my father who had just turned 90. Marcel didn't look a day over 65 and so I wondered what his secret was and what kind of life he had led.

Marcel came into the gallery a few times after that first encounter, and we chatted about many different subjects including the fact that he was also an artist. I was curious about his work and so he invited me to his home to see some of his paintings. In the past, Marcel worked mostly with watercolors, oil paints, and pastels but he could no longer paint with oils due to allergies. He was presently trying to master acrylics, the medium I work with. We chatted companionably, and I listened while he told me a little about his life and his war experiences. He also showed me photos and medals from his service in the RCAF during WWII. We agreed to meet for lunch the following week to continue our conversation.

Coincidentally, my sister was starting to write a novel based on our uncle's life and service as a bombardier in Bomber Command of the RCAF during WWII. Tragically, he was killed in action, so I thought perhaps Marcel might be a valuable resource for my sister's research. Our lunches became a regular event. I became fascinated not only by Marcel's stories of his life during WWII but also those about growing up in northern Alberta on a farm/ranch among ten siblings. I was also intrigued with his recounting of his life after the war. Very quickly I realized that Marcel had an extraordinary memory for detail and a totally engaging storytelling ability. I found that his stories were not only descriptive of the times, poignant, intuitive, funny, occasionally sad and disturbing but presented a unique, personal point of view and a historical record of life in Canada from 1920s to the present time.

Marcel often mentioned that he had a wish to write a book about his life. As I listened, I too believed his life story needed to be written down but not by me. However, I became so drawn into Marcel's very personal revelations about his life that I began to feel a connection to him that I could not explain. It seemed when he was telling me a story, I was right there with him experiencing every moment for myself. Our lunches soon became recording sessions, and an incredible, privileged journey for me began, as Marcel revealed his memories, actions, thoughts, and feelings from a lifetime of 95 plus years. It soon became evident to me that I could never pass this project on to someone else. I felt that compelled to see it through to the finish.

Chapter 2

'Courage is not the absence of fear
but the management of fear.'
– Marcel Croteau

"Of all your dangerous wartime experiences, what do you think was the one that frightened you the most?"

"Well, definitely our mid-air collision would qualify. At approximately 3 a.m. on May 22, 1944, as part of RCAF Bomber Command, the Alouette 425 Squadron was approaching our designated target near Le Mans, France. We were one of approximately 300 bombers on the mission, on edge and pumped to carry out our orders. It was a very hazy night, and the master bomber of the entire group had difficulty locating our target. He ordered each aircraft to orbit in order to give him more time to find the target. To orbit consisted of making four right turns at 90°, flying one minute after the first turn, two minutes after the second turn, one minute after the third turn, and then after the fourth turn, ending up on the original course. Our aircraft proceeded to make the first right turn, flying for one minute and then halfway through the second turn, we were horrified to find the outer part of our starboard wing and motor colliding with one of our own aircraft that had not followed instructions and was in the wrong position.

"I was positioned in the rear turret which was so cramped I had to crawl forward to get into it and crawl backward to get out of it and back into the fuselage of the plane. The rear turret was made of Plexiglas, separated from the fuselage with metal doors. Precariously attached to the back end of the plane meant it wobbled and shook with the vibrations and movement of the fuselage as if it were held in place with bubble gum and duct tape. Depending on the angle that the enemy was approaching from behind, I could rotate the turret to aim precisely at the target. I had to be fast. In that position, I was able to observe any action in a 180-degree arc around me. Because I was facing backward, I was positioned with my four machine guns pointed out in the opposite direction in which we were flying. This meant that I always flew backward and therefore could never see what danger or disaster was occurring ahead of us. My focus was to identify and eliminate the enemy coming toward us from behind. I could let nothing sneak up on us or we would be shot down. However, there was absolutely nothing I could do when I heard and felt a teeth-rattling and bone-jarring bang that signaled a mid-air collision. At the same time, I witnessed the other aircraft pass underneath us. Immediately, our aircraft careened out of control into a flat spin, which is the most deadly of spins. The pilot ordered us to bail out.

I frantically reached behind me with both hands to open my turret doors. There was no room in the turret for a parachute, so it was imperative for me to get back into the fuselage to find my parachute, an impossible 20 feet away. Being the robust farm boy that I was, with great force I grabbed the door handles, pulling them the way they usually opened, but the two handles came off the doors in my hands. They were flimsy aluminum pieces attached to the doors with one rivet each. In order to leave the turret, I usually fell backward into the fuselage from my cramped sitting position. But I now knew I needed to wiggle myself around to face the fuselage and remove my gloves so that with my bare hands I could push the doors off their locked track. Using brute force, to my great relief, the doors finally opened and I crawled forward toward the fuselage of the aircraft. As I wiggled over the door tracks in the floor between the turret and the fuselage, I was terrified to find that the snaps of my parachute harness had caught in the grooves of the track and I was stuck. Frantically, I tore at the snaps and somehow managed to free myself. I crawled into the fuselage but within seconds I passed out because I had undone my oxygen source and my radio connection before leaving the turret. Shortly thereafter, we descended to less than 18,000 feet which meant there was now enough oxygen for me to breathe again, and I regained consciousness. However, the centrifugal force of the spin kept me pinned in that position on the floor. I felt as though my weight must have increased five-fold. Head down, I struggled with all the strength I could muster, on my hands and knees, to make it to my parachute which was securely snapped to the aircraft frame. I was having great difficulty undoing the snaps and I was pinned there. Though success seemed unlikely, I finally freed the snaps just as the centrifugal force decreased which enabled me to shrug into the parachute and fasten it to the harness that I was wearing. Images of my life passed through my mind, and I thought this was it. Those few moments seemed like an eternity.

"Then, I realized that the escape hatch hadn't been opened. I was not passing out so I figured our altitude must be low enough to breathe without an oxygen mask. I had unplugged mine before leaving the turret. The aircraft was still lurching violently but it had come out of the spin. At that moment, I plugged in my intercom and oxygen. I didn't know that the pilot had canceled the bailout order. I asked him what our status was and was told that we were trying to stabilize the aircraft, which seemed to me to be virtually impossible. It kept lurching with the drag of the damaged wing and was always on the verge of stalling and going into another spin. We had to keep the speed at 170 mph or more in order to prevent stalling.

"Carefully, I maneuvered myself back into the turret to take up my duty again. The air stream from the aircraft almost pulled me out of the turret as I rotated it with the doors wide open. We had already descended to approximately 10,000 feet from 20,000 feet, the pilot desperately trying to keep the aircraft at a flying altitude but we continued to lose altitude. Having lost the outer starboard motor in the collision, the pilot had the inner starboard motor at full revolutions to keep it from stalling. He was holding all the controls, the ailerons, and stabilizers against the pull of the stall.

"As was planned, we managed to proceed to the target. I noticed an aircraft burning on the ground. It was later confirmed that it was the one that had collided with us. As we reached the target, luckily its markers were still flaring. We dropped our bombs and optimistically turned to head back to our base in England. By then, the pilot was having even more difficulty holding the aircraft at flying altitude. He asked the crew if we wanted to bail out or risk ditching in the English Channel. With the damage done to one wing and the outer starboard motor, ditching in the ocean was out of the question because we would spin into the water and drown. Bailing out over France was also not an option as the continent was still occupied by the enemy. The thought of being interrogated by the Gestapo and/or the SS was not a good option for any of us.

We all agreed to risk making it back to England on a wing and a prayer with the hope we would live to see another day."

"When you realized your extreme peril, what were you thinking about? Your family, your friends, your girlfriend?"

"All of them."

The Halifax Mark 3 Bombers were in use with most of the 14 Royal Canadian Air Force Squadrons based in Yorkshire England. These aircraft proved to be quite sturdy as this Air Gunner and Crew survived a mid air collision on an occasion while approaching the Target and crash landed on reaching England.

Halifax Mark 3 Bomber

Chapter 3

'In every conceivable manner, the family is a link
to our past and a bridge to our future.'
– Alex Haley

*"You've mentioned in our conversations that your family
has a long history in Canada."*

"My parents' ancestors immigrated to Quebec, Canada, in 1647 from France and became some of the earliest settlers in Canada. Very little changed in their daily lives on the farms they created during those 250 years before my parents were born.

"My maternal grandfather was a skilled craftsman who owned a manufacturing plant in the province of Quebec, near Quebec City. He worked with oak to make very beautiful windows and doors for churches and homes of the wealthy. They were very elaborately crafted and filled with stained glass. In those days, businesses were generally not operated the way they are today. My grandfather took orders for his products in the spring and his employees worked through the remainder of the year fulfilling those orders. During this time, the workers were paid only enough money to cover the cost of clothes and room and board. The remainder of their wages were paid to them when my grandfather received payment upon delivery of the finished windows and doors the following spring.

"One Sunday while my grandfather's family was in church in early March 1908, tragedy struck. My grandfather's youngest brother had behavior problems, a bit like a kid today on drugs only he was stealing alcohol. Although he lived with my grandfather, he was not in church with the rest of the family on that day. There was a big pile of sawdust and shavings on the floor in the factory, and my mother's stepsister, who was just a little girl, saw him set fire to the shavings. Unfortunately, the whole factory burned to the ground destroying all the products finally finished after months of labor.

"Tragically, my grandfather was not going to be paid for the work that went up flames. Therefore, he had no money to pay his employees, no money to pay the suppliers, no factory, just a house. At that time, adventurous or desperate folks, depending on your point of view, were being encouraged by the federal government to help open up Western Canada. For a solution to his difficulties, my grandfather went to the government agency involved and signed up for property in Alberta. Next, he rented a train boxcar for five dollars and planned his family's move west. The family packed their furniture as well as my grandfather's tools and equipment into the boxcar, boarded the train, and set out for the Moose Lake area in Northern Alberta to make a new life for themselves. He had purchased 160 acres or a quarter section for a very minimal sum of money to create a homestead. He became a colonizer of Western Canada, and my family became pioneers once again. As more settlers arrived in the area, a community evolved which was named Bonnyville after the Roman Catholic priest whose name was Bonnin.

"Before the white settlers began arriving, government Indian agents, and surveyors arrived to map out the two reservations that had been created through treaties and also homesteads for the anticipated settlers. The Roman Catholic Church created a presence on the reservation by building a church. A priest named Le Golf was the first missionary priest to arrive. He worked with the two resident tribes and managed to prevent war breaking out between them. Le Golf also gave each person a French Canadian name in an effort to further subdue them. Looking back in history, it is appalling that bad judgment, superiority, greed and politics prevailed in the treatment of our indigenous peoples. It was illegal for them to purchase alcohol; so much later, when they brought freshly caught fish to our home, I hid a jug of wine behind a certain telegraph pole as a form of payment. When I was operating my airline, I made friends with some of the First Nations peoples, many of whom had been in the army during the war. When they were jailed for possession of alcohol, I smuggled beer into the jail for them. In the white communities that grew and developed in the area, there was a lot of prejudice exhibited against the Indians and later against French Canadians, some of which continues to this day.

"My grandfather didn't know anything about land or farming. The land he chose to purchase was on a hill so that he could build his house perched on top. It seemed like a perfect choice. However, the land was still covered with snow, so he could not see all the rocks which needed to be removed. His son, who planned to farm, bought a section just south of his father's which was quite suitable. My grandfather was not a farmer and didn't plan to become one which made his choice of land less problematic. While his wife and children settled into life on the prairies, my grandfather travelled to

Lloydminster to work as a carpenter. All the tools he used were made by him, mainly planes with different chisels giving him the ability to cut edges with different shapes for windows and doors. At age 82 he was still practicing his craft!

"My mother was born in 1897, while the family was still living in Quebec. Her mother died in 1901, when she was only four, making life very tough for her. My grandmother was stricken with tuberculosis so my mother had not been allowed to see her for a long time before she died. This was a devastating experience for a child. She had to cope with hardship and loss before her life had barely begun.

"When my mother was ten years old and just before the family moved out west, her father married a widow with a little girl who soon became my mother's best friend. More children were being born into the family, which meant my mother worked hard, washing diapers with a scrub board and performing other household chores. Owning very few possessions when they arrived in the West meant they had few comforts. Only a sod roof on their hastily constructed house protected them that first year except when deluges of rain dripped in. Because of her heavy workload, there was no time for my mother to attend school. She was a resourceful, intelligent girl who valued education. Somehow she managed to teach herself to speak English and to read and write in French and English.

"As time went on, life for my mother didn't get much better. She was barely 16 years old when she married my father. I think she hoped to escape the drudgery of her life, but she just jumped from the frying pan into the fire. She eventually gave birth to 12 children. Families were discouraged from practicing birth control by the Roman Catholic Church. Priests had a lot of influence over their parishioners. Although my mother had a life full of hard work and drudgery, she lived into her one hundredth year."

*****

"My paternal grandfather owned a mill in St. Patrice, Quebec, which is 50 miles south of Quebec City. The large brick building contained three floors and three turbines and was positioned on a canal. The force of the water flowing over the rapids turned the turbines which then provided the energy to operate the equipment. The ground floor was the sawmill, the middle floor was the feed mill, and the top floor was the flourmill. My grandfather bought the mill from people who lived up river and who controlled the water flow in the canal. They also had a mill to operate and often didn't send enough water down the canal to allow my grandfather to operate his mill. This situation made it a very difficult for him to operate his business.

"When my father was about seven, his father left to go to Dawson City with the intention of improving the family's financial situation. He hoped to achieve great success in the gold rush. My father's older brother was left in charge of operating the mill. My uncle started my father working at six years old in the sawmill. His job was to move the slabs of wood after they had been cut from heavy maple and oak logs. Farmers arrived at the mill with horses and wagons, or sleighs in winter, with their grains for processing into feed or flour. They returned later for the ground product. It was my father's job to fill the bags with the milled grains. Before my grandfather returned from the Yukon, he sent more than $50,000 home, a very large amount of money considering the times. My uncle used that money to remodel the mill.

Unfortunately, his timing was off. Gas motors were becoming available and farmers were starting to mill their own grains with this new equipment. So the business failed. However, the mill is still standing today.

"My grandfather was absent from his family for eleven years. It took six months for him to get to his destination in the Yukon. He purchased 1000 pounds of supplies in Vancouver which he transported by boat up the west coast of British Columbia before heading inland by trekking with other gold seekers over the coastal mountains to the Yukon. After an arduous and dangerous trip on which they were always wary of thieves, he arrived at his destination. For four years my grandfather searched for a good location to pan for gold. Meanwhile he worked in the local assay office. He worked long, difficult, and frustrating hours, but gradually he was rewarded for his efforts and began to regularly send gold home. While he accumulated a shipment, he trusted no one. One night, he was alone in his cabin literally sitting on his stash. A couple of thieves burst into the cabin and demanded that my grandfather hand over his gold, threatening to shoot him if he did not do as he was told. My grandfather didn't own a gun so he just sat there perched on his gold and calmly retorted, ''Go ahead, and shoot me.' The would-be thieves left without another word. He returned home in 1907.

"My father left his home at the mill in St. Patrice at age 14, without an education, and in the middle of winter, on the pretext of wanting to see the color of sand."

"I suppose that was the opposite of those living in a warm climate wanting to see snow."

"Well, perhaps he just wanted a job that paid him cash. There was much more snow than usual that year in Quebec, and although he only had moccasins to wear, he made his way to Maine on foot to work in the lumber camps. Eventually, he left Maine and made the trek west to New Westminster, British Columbia, where an older brother lived. He worked doing odd jobs around that city before moving to Bonnyville, Alberta. There he was able to purchase, for a small amount of cash, a one quarter-section of land which he intended to farm. However, he wasn't quite ready for that so he moved back to Vancouver where he soon decided he did not like digging ditches for a living. Therefore, he returned to Alberta. In 1913, he met and married my mother, who bought another quarter section giving them a total of 320 acres. This allowed my mother to apply for a homestead. Later, they purchased another half-section so they owned 640 acres in total. Part of the property bordered a lake with a sandy beach. However, we never swam there because the cows spent a lot of time in the water avoiding blackflies. There were also lots of bloodsuckers and tiny freshwater shrimp that caught in the cows' hair which we had to brush off when we milked them. All the farmers in the area were pioneers who knew little about farming. My father was raised in a family whose livelihood was a flourmill, so he also knew nothing about farming. However, he was an intelligent man and he learned quickly.

Parents, Anne Marie and Omer Croteau

"The land my parents purchased was all bush. It had to be cleared of cottonwood and poplar trees before a cattle ranch, grain and dairy farm could be developed. The soil was very alkaline, because the land had once been an ancient ocean bottom. When the First Nations occupied the land, they burned the dead grass every spring (the ashes added alkalinity to the soil) to facilitate the growth of new grass on which the wild animals they hunted could feed. When we were clearing the land for crops in the '30s, we found skulls and bones of buffalo. We hung the skulls all over the fences rather than adding them to the rock piles.

wait . . .   *Marcel Croteau*

Marcel's Painting of House

"One section of land purchased by my parents was from another family. There was a one-room cabin on the property next to the road which was the first house in the community built from sawn lumber rather than logs. The kitchen with cupboards, dining area, and all the beds were within one room. The year I was born, the sixth child, Dad bought a bigger house and moved it to the property. It had several bedrooms, a parlor, a large family dining room, and a pantry. The little old house became the kitchen. In 1935, when I was 12 years old, my father built a large addition to our home for our growing family. It had a family room, dining room, separate kitchen, and pantry. The little old kitchen became the space we used to separate the cream from the milk produced by our dairy herd. There was also an icehouse which we nicknamed 'the fridge.' The original house is now situated on the property of the town museum in Bonnyville, Alberta.

"Our family was very large by today's standards. There were 13 of us who needed to be fed, clothed, and housed. A tremendous amount of work was required to operate a large self-sufficient farm where fields of grain and hay were grown, cattle were raised, and cows were milked, not to mention the young children that needed to be cared for. There was always so much work to do, it seemed endless, and no one was exempt from being assigned a job. There was very little time for fun or conversation.

"My family was so uncommunicative that we only found out about a new sibling when my dad came home from the hospital and told us of the new arrival. However, when I was born, my birth was not announced until much later. At 14 months old, my parents took me for the first time to our family home. I felt the strangeness of being with these people I did not know. It was evening and I was nestled in my mother's arms while we rode in a horse-drawn buggy to our destination. I was wrapped in a blanket with a corner of it over my head. The chains on the wheels jangled as they hit rocks in the dirt road. Because I was being taken away by strangers from the only home I knew and from people I loved, naturally I felt abandoned. I have a somewhat vague memory of being carried into an unfamiliar home and being put in an unfamiliar crib made of wood with homemade slats on the sides. It was like a fence around me and it felt odd. Somebody came and pulled my hair. When I was given some food, my four-year-old brother took it away from me. My older siblings were still quite young and I don't think they understood where I suddenly came from. They had lost their youngest brother not long before and now another one had intruded into the family without warning. Possibly, they were just protecting themselves and their positions within the family.

Siblings on First Day Home

"It wasn't until about 15 years ago, when my sister made a comment about my living with my aunt and uncle that disjointed memories started falling into place. It explained why I always felt a very strong bond with my Aunt Aurora. I learned from my sister that my mother had a slow recovery from my birth. She had been diagnosed with cancer during her pregnancy. After my birth, she was treated with radium and spent many months in the hospital. I was sent to live with my aunt and uncle while she regained her health. It seems odd that no one ever mentioned to me that I had spent my infancy with relatives.

"My first clear memory of my father was when my mother took me to visit him where he was out in a field clearing land and burning brush. There was fire still smoldering in the roots that remained underground after cutting the trees down. As we approached, I broke loose from my mother's hand and ran to my father. I was in diapers so I was very young. I can't remember what he said but as I ran across the cinders he grabbed me and put my feet in a pail of water to cool them. Because I hadn't listened to his warnings, he slapped my bum, and from then on our relationship didn't change much. I quickly learned that my father was very strict and seldom talked, but when he said something, you listened and did what he said, period. No discussion! I was uncomfortable with my father for the rest of his life. I felt that he never liked me, much less, loved me.

"In later years, I began to wonder if my absence from the family as an infant inhibited the bonding process between parent and child. It was as though I didn't exist and I had this feeling of not being wanted for most of my life. As a consequence, I hid and held back my emotions. When we were kids, we were always admonished to be good and to behave, even though we might not have felt we did anything wrong. My early impressions of life stayed with me for a very long time with the result that I was self-conscious and did not dare to speak out. Over the years, I've had to do a lot of work on myself to overcome those inhibitions.

"I was the sixth child, the one born before me had passed away from viral jaundice when he was fifteen months old. Therefore, I had three older sisters and an older brother. My sister, who was the third child in order of birth, took care of me when I arrived home after living with my aunt and uncle. She was very strict with me and very bossy, always ordering me around saying, 'Be quiet. Don't say that. Don't say it that way.' She also called me ugly, dumb, evil, and possessed. It was difficult to ignore her because she was the only person who paid any attention to me. Unfortunately, she made trouble in the family until the day she died. However, she did have a good side to her too. It was almost as if she had an evil twin.

And also in her defense, what does a seven-year-old know about child rearing?"

"How did you react to these family dynamics?"

"I can say that I don't remember any happiness at home at all. The result of feeling like I didn't belong in the family was that I worked hard to do my chores, trying to be noticed and appreciated, but it was futile. Nobody ever seemed to pay attention to my efforts. My older brother, by three years, was the exception, always taking credit for my work. He frequently managed to leave me with the manual labor, which I worked diligently to finish. I lost my place as the youngest, 42 months after my birth, when my sister came along and became the apple of my mother's eye. I felt like I had lost my mother. I felt like I had lost everyone."

"Was there ever a time when your mother cuddled you and let you cry in her arms?"

"No, my mother's arms were always too full. When I needed to cry, I would run and hide. There were six siblings that came after me. Probably, others in the family felt left out too, but we never talked about it. It was a Catholic family and everything was supposed to be perfect. There was no complaining because no one had the right to do so. It was a perfection that didn't exist. I was very fearful when I was growing up, mostly because I wasn't allowed to speak. When I said something, there was always one of my older siblings speaking over me, so I learned to be very silent. It was pretty difficult. Even though there were always a lot of people around, I felt very alone. My feelings of loneliness and abandonment would plague me for most of my life. But at least in my teens, I had my dog, named Barney. I knew Barney loved me and I played outside with him, if there was time, when all the chores were done.

"Somehow, we all survived our childhood. My mother lived to be 99, and my father lived to be 95."

"What kind of reward does one get after 75 years of marriage?"

"I think if there is a heaven, they would deserve a place there after years of working hard together and raising 11 children during the worst of times: the Great Depression and WWII."

The Croteau Family

Chapter 4

'If I stay angry, that anger will take away
my soul, my love and my heart.'
– Marcel Croteau

"It sounds like you had a very difficult time growing up. You said you felt abandoned at other times as well. How did that come about?"

"When we came home from the war, after our participation in combat, I believe a lot of the veterans, myself included, felt like we were in a foreign country. For many reasons our experiences overseas were not to be talked about, even among ourselves. No one wanted to acknowledge the horrors of war, much less talk about them. It was like walking around with a big black cloud hanging over my head, a feeling I'd had ever since I was a child. Only now the cloud was much bigger.

"I returned home from the war by ship in January 1945. RCAF rear air gunners were positioned on the lower level of the ship where we managed the artillery equipment. We were on constant watch. The war was not yet over, and we were very worried about possible attacks by the German U-boats. All the way from Grenoch to New York, there were always two of us, four hours on and four hours off, operating anti-aircraft and anti-submarine artillery, hoping to avoid any confrontation with the enemy.

"Making our way across the Atlantic Ocean to New York, our route took us through the Bermuda Triangle where we ran into a vicious winter storm. This was a new experience for me, having grown up on the Prairies where our storms were on solid footings. Although the ship was 770 feet long, it pitched in the heavy seas like a toy boat. Waves poured over the deck threatening to wash us into the sea where we could soon become fish food. We desperately clung to the steel handrails as we tried to make our way into the cabin and to what we hoped would be relative safety. Inside, the ship pitched from the trough to the crest of each wave. This created a nauseating motion as we climbed upwards through the passageways, and then braced ourselves to prevent falling forward as the ship dropped downwards. It was like trying to walk on a teeter-totter.

"Not soon enough, we arrived in New York Harbor. From there, we traveled by train to Quebec City, where I spent a few days with family before boarding another train that took me to Montreal, then Edmonton, and finally to Bonnyville, Alberta. I had hoped I would be able to further my education when I arrived home from the war, but for many reasons, including marriage, it was not to be. Needless to say, I was not prepared for the difficulties I encountered. There was no place for veterans. We were generally treated as if we were just taking up space. It was difficult to comprehend our reception. I came from a French Canadian town that was full of guys that had not gone to war. I suspect they were fearful of us because of what we had experienced and what they had missed. I also think they thought that because we came home as war heroes, we could accomplish things on our own. Because my accomplishments during the war were substantial and well known, the pressure to succeed that, I felt, caused me much stress and anxiety.

Little did anyone know how damaged we were from what we had seen and what we had done.

"The priest in our town was French Canadian and his family had come originally from Brittany. He was totally against our participation in the war and he was not alone."

"One would have thought he would support fighting to liberate France since there lay his roots."

"On the contrary, his attitude was: '*C'etait un affair d'Anglaise.*' Many others had the same opinion. Initially, there was some fanfare when I arrived home and a party was held for me. There were men with bagpipes along with the Chamber of Commerce at the train station to greet me when I arrived home, but what I really wanted most of all was to find my family. When I spotted them, my older brother was conspicuously absent. Nevertheless, I broke through the crowd and raced to them. I had made it home!!!"

"Once the dust settled, I guess reality set in for you."

"It seemed like no one would give us any support when we began the onerous task of trying to adjust to civilian life. I felt totally abandoned and misunderstood. It was like fighting the war, albeit a different kind of war, all over again. Before we left Europe, the Air Force's idea of adjustment to civilian life was for us to return home and get married. After arriving home, I wanted to go see my sisters in California, but my girlfriend wasn't about to go with me without a ring on her finger. Within seven days, we married. At least I fulfilled that part of the advice given to me. My new wife and I were young and hardly knew each other, which didn't bode well for our future. The DVA (Department of Veterans Affairs) offered loans which were helpful to those wanting to purchase a farm or get an education. I came home from the war expecting to purchase a farm with the $5,000 loan offered by the DVA. One of the consequences of the Great Depression was that I learned the benefits of living on the farm. From1928 to 1932, we had a parade of people at our door looking for food, shelter, and work. I knew that no matter what happened, on the farm we would always have abundant supplies of food and a roof over our heads. The practical part of me wanted to continue the family tradition of farming, and my wife was a farm girl, so it seemed like the natural thing to do. However, there was a part of me I hardly recognized, that knew that was really not the life I wanted. Instead, I took a job working for Case Farming Equipment in Bonnyville. After the war, they had only one tractor to sell, not much opportunity for success there!

"My wife and I rented a house in Bonnyville and proceeded to set up housekeeping. Initially, we paid rent of $13.50 a month. When the wartime rent controls were removed, our rent was raised to $17.50. Unknown to me, my wife and her sister went to the rent control board and complained about the rent increase. Our landlord immediately put our two-bedroom house up for sale. It quickly sold for $750.00, so we had to look for another place to live. This established a pattern of behavior by my wife throughout our marriage. Another nail in the coffin of our relationship.

"Perhaps, it was just the French Canadian community that I lived in, but few doors opened for me. On the contrary, it seemed as though there was very little acceptance for war veterans. After all, we had been fighting a war to help the English Protestants, hardly something a French Canadian Catholic should do. They simply didn't know how to behave around us, much less a decorated officer like me. Some tried intimidation and aggression which ended in a few fights. I was very strong and had learned some physical combat maneuvers while in training for the military, so I had the upper hand. That did not help the situation.

"What no one understood, at that time, was that although we were returning home seemingly whole, albeit some of us had visible physical injuries, we were trying to integrate into a society that had even less insight into our mental and emotional injuries than we did. After all, we were still just kids. Everyone expected that we would just fall back into the lives we had left as though nothing had happened to us. It felt like being abandoned again, and I was on my own to figure it all out. Of course, that was impossible.

"Much later, I realized that I should never have returned home to Bonnyville."

Article's highlighting Marcel's Achievements

DISTINGUISHED FLYING MEDAL

R197075 Sgt. Joseph Marcel Albert Croteau, R.C.A.F., No. 425 (R.C.A.F.) Sqdn. (Bonnyville, Alta.).

As rear gunner, this airman has participated in several sorties, including attacks on such targets as Essen, Frankfurt and Karlsruhe. During the attack on the last-named target his aircraft was engaged by a fighter. Sgt. Croteau used his guns with deadly effect, however, and his bullets set the enemy aircraft on fire. It fell to the ground and exploded on impact. His skill and determination were characteristic of that he has shown on all occasions.

Croteau receives his DFM ring off an enemy fighter and attacked his bomber to is Karlsruhe. Croteau used a gens to good effect, the fighter on fire. It off to fall to the ground, t exploded on impact.

Avion nazi désintégré

Je n'oublierai jamais ce spectacle, raconte un mitrailleur canadien-français.

Par Maurice Desjardins

correspondant de guerre des journaux de langue française

Avec le C.A.R.C. en Angleterre, b (P.C) — "En une seconde, dit le sergent Marcel Croteau, de Bonnyville, Alberta, j'ai vu la désintégration de mon avion nazi à mitrailleuses, de pratique et de tir."

Croteau, mitrailleur arrière d'un Halifax de l'escadrille Alouette, revenait de décembre en du 30 au-dessous de Karlsruhe.

"Je n'oublierai jamais le spectacle de la désintégration de ce chasseur ennemi," dit-il.

L'avion de Croteau est piloté par le sergent de section Jean-Paul Lavallée, de Magog, et le navigateur est le sous-officier breveté Elliott Falchault, de Montréal.

"Il était une heure du matin, raconte Croteau, j'aperçus au avion nazion à 300 mètres. En un coup l'oeil, il était à portée de tire en meilleures. J'ouvris le feu, saisis le langage. Je vis mes balles traînantes se loger dans le moteur droit du Junkers. En quelques secondes l'avion ennemi prit feu et disparut dans une terrible explosion."

HELP FRENCH LIBERATION — These aircrew lads of the Alouette Squadron in R.C.A.F. Bomber Group Overseas are smiling because they have just returned from a successful bombing raid in the invasion area the night after D-Day. Their bombs helped to destroy a German used railway bridge. Looking over the invasion map table back at their station are, left to right: Flight Sgt. J.E.N. Lurin, 564 Des Ormeaux St., Montreal, bomb aimer; Flight Sgt. Paul Lavallée, Magog, Que., pilot; Sgt. J.M. Croteau, D.F.M. Bonnyville, Alta., rear gunner. For all three it was their 15th trip.

Heureux et fiers de hâter la libération de la France, leur mère-patrie, ces trois aviateurs canadiens-français, qui font partie de l'escadrille des Alouettes" refont sur la carte géographique l'itinéraire qu'ils ont suivi pour bombarder la zone d'invasion, le lendemain soir du débarquement allié sur les plages de France. Leur mission consistait à détruire un pont de chemin de fer utilisé par les boches. De gauche à droite: le sergent de section J.-E.-N. Lurin, bombardier, 564, rue Desormeaux, Montréal; le sergent de section Paul Lavallée, de Magog (Qué.), pilote; et le sergent J.-M. Croteau, D.F.M., mitrailleur arrière, de Bonnyville (Alta). Tous trois en étaient à leur quinzième raid. (C.A.R.C.)

Chapter 5

'In the city one works until quitting time.
On the farm one works until the job is done.'
– Marcel Croteau

"Marcel, the first story you ever told me was about the mid-air collision which I want to get back to, but I'm very curious about your life before that pivotal event. You were born in 1923. What was it like living through a time in history, on the Canadian prairies, that was so full of hardship and uncertainty?"

"At 5:30 a.m. we struggled out of bed. In winter, it could be as cold as 40° F below zero outside. The fire in the kitchen stove, our main source of heat, routinely died overnight. We usually slept two in a bed to keep warm. There were four bedrooms upstairs. The girls' rooms contained a double bed and a single bed. The brothers had one bedroom with mattresses on the floor. The mattresses were filled with straw that had to be changed regularly, yet another chore to be accomplished. Because we were so young, pulling the straw out of the mattress and refilling it was very difficult. The animals ate the used straw, so we wasted nothing.

"As soon as we got up in the morning, we had to move fast, a *'va vite'* admonishment from our mother ringing in our ears. It was so cold in winter, when we climbed out of our

41

warm beds, that we were shivering and shaking until we put on our clothes. Dad was lighting the stove as we came downstairs, but there was no time to stop and warm up by the fire.

"We raced to the barn to start work right away. It was not much colder outside than it was inside the house. Fortunately, our physical activity caused our chilled blood to flow again through our young bodies. Our first priority was to care for the calves and the cows. We cleaned the floors, put down fresh straw, and fed them, then we milked each cow by hand. Two hours of work was completed before we went to school. We were not supervised so we had to manage our own time, making sure we could squeeze in breakfast between completing our chores and leaving for school. As we grew older, our assigned chores would change and new skills were learned. There was a hierarchy of positions for the eleven children and we each learned to do various chores.

"When the depression hit, in 1929, I was just turning six, the magical age in our family for beginning our roles as child slave laborers. It was the end of my childhood, as all hands were required to manage the large farm. During the depression, there was no longer a market for beef or grain. One of our most valuable cattle would sell for only four dollars! The only real income available to us was from milking cows and selling the cream to the local creamery for churning into butter. This created a lot of work for me and my siblings. We were milking up to 20 cows twice a day by hand.

"Running water was non-existent. This meant we had to haul water in pails from the wells for household needs and for the barn. Water was hand pumped into troughs for the cattle and horses. Eventually, we had flywheels with gas motors that pumped water down a trough, which was attached to the pump and made of jack pine, into storage tanks. Many farmers were still using windmills to pump water. We used kerosene lamps for light. They had to be cleaned regularly and refilled with fuel. In 1952, electricity was installed on the farm after the lines were installed next to the road.

"The toilet facility was only for the female members of the family. Males had to use the barn in winter and the outhouse in the summer. The outhouse had two holes, one large and the other one small, to accommodate all sizes in the family. In those days, the Eaton's catalogue performed double duty. When it became out of date, Mother removed all the pages with images of feminine undergarments before she discarded the catalogue for use in the outhouse. The softer pages were always used first.

"All the farming was done by horse-drawn handmade implements. Nothing was mechanized. We learned to ride horses by the time we were four years old and by six years old, to drive them. By the time I was seven years old, during the summer, I used a team of horses to rake the freshly mowed hay into bunches. Then two teams, with two horses each, were hitched to a bucking pole with which I used to haul the hay into haystacks in the field. This job could be messy enough to require more raking. Eventually, I could handle a ton of hay every twenty minutes. As my skill level increased and I grew older, I was promoted to more difficult operations of the farm. Stooking grain was another job that increased my strength and stamina. In my early teens, I could drive eight horses on the plow, or work with a team of four horses in each hand with the binder in order to form the sheaves of grain in the fields. Then we stooked the sheaves of grain by hand. A stook is an arrangement of sheaves, or bundles of cut grain stalks, arranged much like a teepee to keep grain heads of wheat, barley or oats off the ground. The grain would dry, or cure, before it was collected for threshing, which is the removal of grain from the stalks.

"Because we grew all of our own food, we were always well fed. In the morning we ate porridge with cream and sugar and then ate a sandwich for lunch at school. When we returned home, at the end of the school day, we didn't eat until suppertime around 7:00 p.m. My older sisters, who worked in the house, did a large portion of the cooking. They wouldn't allow us to eat when we got home from school, worrying that we would spoil our appetite for dinner. By dinnertime, later in the evening after our chores were finished, we were famished. We were served a big meal with lots of red meat and vegetables. Our family didn't eat much pork, although in summer, we ate salt pork occasionally. We had a smokehouse where we smoked hams and ribs. Large crocks held pork bellies which my mother covered with brine to create bacon. She also used these large crocks to make pickles. The lids of the crocks frequently got broken, so she replaced them with sheets of tin salvaged from old signs.

"Beef was our first choice of meat. There were no electric refrigerators in those days, but we did have an icehouse. In the summer, we stored meat and cream in pails hung down our well which still had some ice in it long after winter had passed. In the early spring, our beef which was stored in the icehouse was still frozen, but would soon thaw. Therefore, my mother canned it in half-gallon jars for storage until it was needed. It was very delicious, stewed, roasted, or cooked on the top of the stove. For one of my favorite meals, my mother cut the beef into steaks about one quarter inch thick and had a hot pan and butter ready to quickly fry them. There was no such thing as a barbeque. To make gravy, she poured fresh cream into the pan.

The steaks and gravy were then served with potatoes, carrots and other root vegetables, salt and pepper. The meal was delicious.

"In the summer, I worked in the garden with my mother. When I was quite young, one of my jobs was to weed our large cornfield. After a day of hard work in the fields, one night I consumed 22 cobs of fresh buttered and salted corn. From our large crop of corn, my mother canned big jars of corn on the cob. In the winter, we would savor this corn all the more because of the labor required to preserve it. Another treat was freshly baked bread served with freshly churned butter, the only kind we ever had. In those days, the bread was snowy white, no grains or husks in sight. It was a sign of prosperity, the whiter the better."

"Did your mother grind your flour?"

"No, there was a flour mill in St. Paul's about 45 miles away, where once a year we took some of our grain to be milled. After 1930, there was a mill located nearby that milled our grain. It was made into flour, cream of wheat and bran, which was mixed with oats to make porridge. We always ate well and plentifully. Because everyone worked so hard, we really could burn the calories. Weight gain was never a problem. None of us had an ounce of fat on us. When I was at boot camp, someone asked what gym I worked out in. My answer was: the farm.

"When I had time off, on a Sunday afternoon, I would go out with my dog into the forest to hunt grouse, prairie chickens, ducks, and rabbits. In the winter, there was deep snow which made my hunting more challenging. I walked along with my dog Barney, carrying a pole and snare, half a mile or so from the house to my favorite hunting spot. At this time, I was not old enough to have a gun but looked forward to being allowed to use one when I turned ten. Barney and I knew exactly where to go to find the partridges and we had a routine for hunting. The dog would run ahead of me, and as soon as he found them, he would bark. If I didn't have the dog with me, I barked to distract the birds while I prepared the snare. I would climb the trunk of a large old willow tree trunk in order to snare the partridge. If I climbed slowly, I could easily capture one. The poor bird. I wouldn't do it now, but it was a different time then.

Every year in the fall, thousands of ducks, on their way south for the winter, passed over our farm and flew by overhead for at least an hour and a half, quacking and filling the sky until it was black with no light filtering through. If they stopped to have lunch in our fields, they were capable of destroying whole crops. We shot at the waterfowl mostly to scare them away.

"One of my brothers had a bladder problem and frequently wet the straw mattress we slept on. Once a month, it was my responsibility to take the straw out of its cover and add it to the used straw pile. I gave the cover to Mother who laundered it in the wringer washing machine and then hung it outside to dry. When it was dry, I took the clean cover back to the straw pile, filled it with new clean straw, and then carried the mattress on my hunched back to the house. Our big bull was usually standing out in the pasture, and I was scared as hell, having him scrutinize me so closely. I noticed too that there was something that the cows were staring at, that was making them excited, or at least as excited as a cow can get. Eventually, I realized it was me they were watching. This big white thing on my back and my skinny little legs moving along underneath was the source of their anxiety. Fortunately, I had my dog with me for protection."

"Where was your older brother?"

"In all of this, he would never be around. He was Dad's favorite. It seemed to me that I performed most of the dirty chores. However, all the kids were engaged in performing chores, of one kind or another, by the time we turned six.

"I remember before I started school I had a stool, like a high chair, that I used to sit on to help my mother with the endless laundry. We had a wringer washer that had a gear which needed to be turned back and forth to agitate the clothes in the water. That was my job, to help my mother who had so much work to do. There was very little play in my life.

"It was the children who milked the cows, starting at six in the morning. Our dairy cows numbered about 20, though usually more in the summer. They had to be milked twice a day. We each had three or four cows to milk in the morning before school and again at night before bed. The cows were loose, with the bull among them, in the corral that was attached to the barn. We each had a little stool and a pail, which we carried as we went from cow to cow. They liked to move around in the corral, and I had one cow that liked to walk all around the enclosure before she came back to her place. I had to follow behind her. Otherwise, she would stop and not be in a position where I could milk her. It was torture until we finished. Our job was to feed the animals as well. We chopped oats and gave a gallon pail to each milking cow twice a day. As well, we looked after the young calves, feeding them milk to drink also twice a day. We hauled the milk from the barn into the milk house every morning and every night where the milk and cream were separated. Then we took the leftover milk back to the calves in the barn. We did this day and night. In the evening, all the utensils were steam boiled to sanitize them for the use the next morning.

We were suffering through the Depression. There was no money to be earned from the milk these cows produced, but we sold about three or four eight-gallon cans of cream every week. At home, we always enjoyed the excess fresh cream because after two days of storage, it was no longer saleable. We made our deliveries of cans of cream to the creamery in town three miles from where we lived. In the summer, we used the horse and buggy for transportation. The cans were covered with horse blankets over which we poured cold water. This kept the cream cool during the trip from the icehouse, where the cream was stored, to the creamery. It was a lot of physical activity. We delivered on Friday, Monday, and Wednesday, going in the direction opposite to the way we went to school. This wasn't very convenient during school months. We were paid $2.10 for an eight-gallon pail of cream, not the expected 33% butterfat, but an astounding 44%. Because the cream was held on ice, it always tested as high quality. Sometimes, we would send cream by train to Edmonton, to Woodlands Dairy, where they made ice cream with it. They often sent us letters requesting our cream because of its high quality. Sometimes, if I had too much other work to do, my younger sister went with my father to the creamery. Everyone had to participate in the work involved on a large farm with a large family. There was never a shortage of chores. Each one of us had to do his share.

"We had a wooden ice-cream maker that we filled with ice and salt and then added cream to the inner compartment. It was hard work churning the cream but the end result was heavenly! We often shared our ice cream with friends and family. One hot summer day, my younger brother who was 12 or 13 at the time, churned a full container of ice cream then went and hid while he ate the whole thing!"

"What breed of cows did you have?"

"We had Shorthorn cows that were usually raised as beef cattle but we also used them as dairy cows. They were certainly not as productive as Jersey or Holstein dairy cows. Shorthorns were so hard to milk that my hands and wrists became very strong. From each of the two milkings per day, each cow only gave one pail that was about 24 inches high, but it was very rich milk. Most farmers, who had dairy cows, had part Jersey or part Ayrshire breeds. None of our immediate neighbors had dairy cows. They were grain farmers. We were the only ones in the vicinity who had a dairy, beef and grain operation, probably because there was not much of a market for milk. In addition, Holstein calves would sell for very little for the beef. This made Shorthorn beef cattle better choice for us because there was a market for the calves to be raised for beef. My mother at one time came up with the idea to breed a Shorthorn with a Jersey, but we ended up with neither a good source of milk nor marketable beef so that ended that experiment.

Shorthorn Cow

"Animal husbandry was something that farmers didn't talk about, but it was very important on the farm. In order to keep up milk production, there were always cows delivering calves. After giving birth, the cow would produce milk for a few months, then her milk supply would dry up. After giving birth to another calf, she would start producing milk again and the cycle would continue. We had to be aware of what was happening with each pregnant cow and be available to help with the birth when needed. The cows weighed up to 1,800 pounds. My dad and I worked as a team to help the cow with the birth. He acted as the veterinarian. If she was in trouble, we helped her give birth by tying a rope around the front legs of the calf and gently pulling on the rope to ease it out of its mother. We delivered many, many, calves but I don't remember ever losing one. When a calf was born, for the first three or four days, we would let the calf suckle its mother so that it could get the quality of milk that would help build its immune system and develop its stomach. We milked the extra left in the mother to give to the older calves. The skim milk, left over from the cream extraction, was also given to the calves in small pails, which were held up to their noses for them to drink. Their enthusiastic drinking left big red marks where the pail that gouged their little faces.

"At the end of the day, all we wanted to do was to go to bed and not think about the next morning. We just wanted to sleep. Because we worked two hours in the morning and up to four hours at night, after school, we rarely had the time or energy to do homework.

"As I think about it right now, it's like I'm experiencing my childhood all over again. The kids today likely wouldn't understand how different life was for me as a child. At the time, we didn't know anything about the world beyond the little community in which we lived, although occasionally, a Montreal Gazette was available to read, at least for those who could read. We were accustomed to the way we were raised. We were tested for our brawn, not our brains. It's a totally different world out there now."

"Yes. Milk comes from the supermarket now, doesn't it?"

"I can remember when I was a little kid, before I started school, I went with my dad to get ice in early spring. The ice would be stored in the icehouse for use during the warm weather. We had to cut blocks of ice from the lake that bordered our farm. This lake was about six miles long and one and a half miles across. We chose an area of the lake where the water was so deep the ice measured about three feet thick. In early March, equipped with ice saws, we made a hole in the ice so Dad could put the saw into it and make two cuts. Then, he made two more cuts, perpendicular to the first cuts, to create a large block of ice. We wrapped a chain around the block and our team of horses was hitched to that chain to pull the huge chunk of ice out of the lake. With a chisel, my dad cut the large blocks into smaller more manageable sizes in order to move the ice blocks onto the sleigh. Dad had devised a system using a chute which looked like a trough with no ends. With the horses stationed by the side of the chute, the block of ice was chained from either side to the horses who then dragged the ice up the chute where Dad positioned it on the sleigh using large ice tongs. In those days, everything was done by hand. One had to be resourceful. The blocks of ice were taken back to the farm where they were stored inside the icehouse, covered with a thick layer of sawdust. We used the sawdust for insulation, so that the ice would last for months. The sawdust was brushed off when the ice was required for use. Enough ice was stored to meet our needs throughout the summer and into the fall.

"My father liked animals, especially horses, and he was very good with them. It seemed at times that he treated them better than his children. Our horses were very important to our farming operations. We loved, valued, and respected them. I did what I could to make sure they were well taken care of. They were watered and fed four times a day, three times with oats. I brushed them well and washed them making sure that they were clean underneath their collars. We put a little bleach in the water to disinfect their skin if there were any abrasions.

"It was necessary to keep the horses' hooves well-manicured so that they could maintain their grip on the dirt roads. I learned how to shoe horses by watching my dad. The inside of the hoof had to be cleaned out and the rest scraped and trimmed to make sure no edges would hang over the metal shoe. The shoe was then nailed to the hoof with special horseshoe nails."

"How did the horses react to the shoeing? Were they patient?"

"Of course. We all had to be patient. The horse probably weighed about 1,600 pounds, so we had to be careful. We held the foot and hoped the horse wouldn't decide to put his foot down, all the while talking quietly and gently with him until he was comfortable with the process. Dad was very skilled at shoeing horses and also was a good teacher.

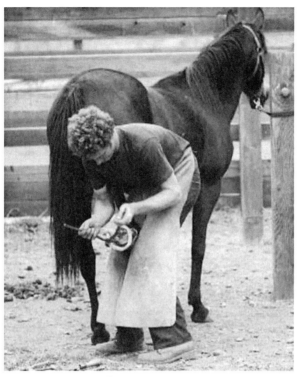

Shoeing Horses

"When I was a teenager, I often worked in the fields with two teams of four horses, one team controlled by each hand. When I came to the end of the row in the field, I needed to turn in a U shape to work the next row. The team of four horses in the inside of the turn needed to move more slowly and take small steps. The team on the outside of the turn had to take quicker, longer steps. The fastest horses were in front so that they could lead the others. Each horse was connected individually to a rein, and I held four of these reins in each of my hands between my five fingers. A signal from me to each horse, as if each one was a limb on a marionette, instructed them how to move. I also used verbal commands. This process directed all the horses to harmonize their movements so that together we could efficiently make a turn in the field. It was like a military drill, or perhaps more like an intricately choreographed dance, with everybody in the right position, making the right moves at the right time.

"I learned a lot about managing animals through plowing, harrowing, seeding, discing, and mowing, all of which required horse power. I had to be agile, physically and mentally, to get each horse to perform as required. The skills I learned and the experiences managing two teams of four horses simultaneously would soon prove to be a very valuable."

Chapter 6

'I enlisted in the RCAF because I wanted to fly,
escape the farm and have a holiday!'
– Marcel Croteau

"There are always any number of reasons why young men and women enlist in the armed forces. Number one: to fight for a cause, number two: to get a job or an education, number three: to find adventure and travel, number four: to be patriotic, or in your case: to escape from an intolerable life and to fulfill a long held dream."

"I would say that most of us, enlisting for combat in World War II, really didn't have any idea what we were getting into. After all, we were just kids. I was barely 19. Ever since I was a young child and watched Grant McConachie (CEO of Canadian Pacific Airlines) buzz over my elementary school with his plane, my persistent and overwhelming desire was to fly. For me, joining the Air Force would be my chance to spread my wings in more ways than one. The prospect of getting away from the farm and doing something new with my life was intoxicating.

"Reinforcement of my plan to enlist came from an unlikely source: my father's behavior toward me for most of my life. I felt like an indentured servant in my family, unwanted, and unloved. On Saturday nights, my father paid my older brother ten dollars and my younger one five dollars. He told my brothers to give me some of their money, but they never did. I asked my mother once for some money which she willingly gave to me, but I felt so guilty that I gave it back to her. Her need for money seemed greater than mine.

"Several months before enlisting, I started looking elsewhere for a job, but only after our barn was filled with hay for use during the encroaching winter. I approached two farmers. One I knew, the other one I didn't really want to work for because he was my girlfriend's father. I was thrilled to land a job where I was paid $30 a month for my work which was a new experience for me. I packed my things in a sack, walked out the door, and across the fields to freedom. My father watched me go but never said a word.

"After a few months of employment, I summoned the courage in, June 1942, to write a letter to the recruiting office in Edmonton in which I requested enlistment into the RCAF. Shortly afterwards, I was sent a train ticket from the recruiting office to travel from Bonnyville to Edmonton. For me to go away on my own, to be interviewed by the military, was a very exciting but also a scary event. I was just a farm boy! What did I know? Well, what I did know was that I would have to have a medical examination and since I had never had one before I was very nervous that I might not pass the tests. That was a needless worry.

During one of my aptitude tests, my inability to train as a wireless operator using Morse code was revealed. To my relief, the captain informed me that I didn't qualify for the job. I had too many problems with the dits and dots. It was my last choice for a position in the Air Force, so I was happy. I was pleased when it was decided that I had the aptitude to be a rear air gunner, which I much preferred anyway. There were IQ tests, which were easy on me, although I don't remember them in any detail. The important thing was to pass, and that was all I wanted. At that time, the Air Force didn't have an immediate opening for a rear gunner, so I was sent back home to wait until a course was available for me.

"My cousin was living and working in Bonnyville at that time. I lived with him while waiting to be called up. The mail came three times a week, and I anxiously checked at the post office whenever there was a delivery. Finally, one day, I got a message that the RCAF was ready for me, two stressed-filled months after I had enlisted. I was required to fill out a form and send it right back to the recruiting office the next morning. I bought a train ticket and immediately left for Edmonton with great excitement and some apprehension.

"I didn't want to worry my parents, so I had not yet told them what I was doing. When I was called to report for training, I had been gone from home for several months. At that point, I had to tell them about my plans. Their reaction was not good. It was well known that the longevity of many airmen was short, about 20% survived the war. A story was circulating that a gunner during WWI lived for seven minutes. There was also the knowledge that during the Battle of Britain, July 10, 1940 to October 31, 1940, Bomber Command suffered huge losses. People met with my parents and asked them why they let me enlist. Did they know I was not going to survive the war? This was followed by further admonishments to my parents for not preventing me from going. They blamed my parents and yet they really didn't know anything about my situation. French Canadians in northern Alberta were generally not in favor of the war. A priest at the time, who was a native of Brittany, was against participation in the war. This seemed very odd because by then France was occupied by the

Germans. There were a lot of zombies (draft dodgers) among French Canadians. They claimed to be farmers during the war to justify their staying at home; but after the war, most of them were businessmen and professionals."

"Did anyone else object to your going to war?"

"My third older sister, from her exalted position as a nun, took every opportunity to advise my parents. She was very disappointed when she found out I had enlisted. It seemed as though my family was taking one more opportunity to disagree with my choices, but in reality, they may very well just have been worried that I would not return home from the war. Nevertheless, it was what I wanted to do. The prospect was exciting and I loved every minute that I was in the Air Force. It was my chance to do something for me."

Photo taken by the royal Family Photographer,Wallace
Heaton December, 1944

Chapter 7

'Life is a learning process.
I rebelled a lot against that learning.'
– Marcel Croteau

"When I turned six, I started school in September of 1929. They found out I was coming and the stock market crashed! My brothers and sisters usually traveled the three miles to school in a horse-drawn buggy or on one of our horses. When riding on horseback, I usually rode seated behind my brother. I sat behind the saddle and bounced along, which of course gave me a really sore bum afterwards. However, on my very first day of school, I rode by myself on our horse Old Blue. On the way to school, my older brother was way ahead of me because he rode a younger and faster horse. We had about two dozen horses on the farm, but Old Blue was always my favorite. I remember vividly the joy that he brought to my young life. He was a beautiful horse, with a beautiful mane, bluish in color with a few white hair, indicative of his 24 years. I loved that old horse. He listened to me as he looked at me with his large brown eyes, set in a white face outlined with dark lines.

"I learned to ride Old Blue, who was a family pet, when he was in our yard eating grass, his usual place to graze. However, if Blue ever went missing, we always knew we could go to the school and find him grazing on the school property. He was very tall, and I was very young, probably about four years old, so I had to figure out how I could climb up on him. I eventually worked out that if I could get close to his face when his head was down munching grass, I would be able to grab his ears and wrap my legs around the lower part of his head. This immediately caused him to raise his head, which then allowed me to grab his mane and pull myself up onto his back, where I sat comfortably, as he continued to graze. I was sitting backward but that was good training for me for my future career as a rear gunner in the RCAF.

Because we were so young when we learned to ride a horse, we always rode bareback because my father would not let us use saddles until we were much older. A terrible accident precipitated my father's decision. My cousin's foot got caught in his saddle's stirrup as he fell off the horse he was riding. The horse had suddenly bolted sideways after being startled by some sheep that moved in the underbrush which lined the perimeter of a field. Tragically, my cousin died of his injuries.

Marcel at the family Farm (far right),Bonnyville, Alberta, Fall 1930

61

"On my first day at school, as we rode across a meadow into some woodlands, the air was filled with the fragrance of high bush cranberries, a sign of the end of summer. My schoolbag thumped against my back, as I rode through the school gate, anticipating the beginning of a new chapter in my life. When I look back to when I started school, I should have stayed home! This school was horrible because our teacher had no tolerance for kids, especially the younger ones. There were eight grades in one room with one teacher. Inevitably, the teacher didn't have time to attend to all of us, so he assigned a 15-year-old student to teach the youngest children math. Unfortunately, in spite of the kid's age, he could neither read nor write, much less do math. For example, to teach us the basics in math, he held two cards, each with a number on one side, and asked us to add the numbers together. This guy didn't know the answers so he always called on an older boy in the class, usually my cousin Paul, who inevitably and purposefully gave a wrong answer. The poor 'substitute' teacher didn't know the answers were written on the back of the cards. I didn't learn any math that year!

Although he knew it would be difficult to find a replacement teacher during the depression on the prairies, my father complained to the school board about the quality of instruction being offered at the school. My father thought, if his children were going to go to school, they were not going to waste their time drawing in a scribbler and sharpening pencils, activities which frequently got me dragged by my ear to the corner in the front of the classroom. Each time, I spent the remainder of the day there on my knees. Eventually, our teacher was fired. Later he became a judge, hopefully a more suitable position for him. At Easter, Gabrielle Roy's sister became our new teacher.

"Throughout the year, I sat in the back of the classroom, beside my 15-year-old 'math teacher.' He was a bully, and there were two or three of us who had to sit with him, on the bench behind our common desk. I don't remember how the others behaved around me, but I remember how he behaved. He would wrap his hands around my neck and squeeze as hard as he could. He also liked to pinch my leg. If I yelped, he stopped. However, the teacher, who didn't see his behavior, reprimanded me for the noise I made and once again sent me to the corner. I was confused by the injustice of it all, and wondered if this was to be my future at school: kneeling in the corner. As it turned out, being bullied at home and at school, which I found both intimidating and humiliating, became a pattern of behavior from others toward me for a large part of my life.

"Only after completing our morning chores was it okay to prepare for school. After carrying the cans of milk to the icehouse after cream separation, we ran into the house for breakfast. If we didn't have time to complete separating the cream, we were treated to porridge with milk that was so thick you could hardly pour it and thick slices of homemade bread. That was our breakfast which was followed by a mad dash to the horses and a fast ride to school. In spite of our haste and our best efforts, we were usually late, for which we were reprimanded. I tried to think of excuses to explain to the teacher why we had not arrived on time but I couldn't say that we had to milk the cows before coming to school. We protected our parents because good Catholic children never put their parents in a bad light. That was the philosophy of the day. Times have changed. Thankfully, expecting a child today to work two hours before school and three or four hours after school is no longer acceptable.

"By the time I spent the day in school, completed my chores for the morning and evening, and ate dinner at 7 p.m., I didn't have the energy to do my homework. I couldn't even think of opening a book, I was that dead tired. Fortunately, I have a good memory and I remembered everything the teacher said."

"Well you do have a wonderful memory for details. I don't doubt that you remembered everything you heard."

"That good memory frequently got me into trouble with my girlfriends because I remembered everything they said. There were often conversations they didn't want to be reminded of.

"I rarely did homework because my older sisters had the one and only kerosene lamp. There was another light in the kitchen that came from a small lamp on a wall bracket with a little reflector. I couldn't see very well with it. The whole situation was not conducive for me to do my homework. On my way to school, I spent a great deal of time trying to conjure up excuses to give the teacher for my incomplete homework. I could never come up with a very good excuse. Naturally, my marks also were not very good."

"Was your teacher cognizant of your situation at home regarding your homework?"

"We didn't explain anything. We were good Catholic kids who expected to be closely observed but not listened to. I was a child trying to be accepted. By grade six, I think my teacher passed me in order not to have me in her class the next year. I moved on to another school where, in February of 1936, my teacher asked me why I didn't work more diligently. I took her advice and applied myself. To my surprise, I came in first with my marks. However, I soon fell back into my old habits and just managed to pass grade seven and eight."

"You have talked about many of your difficulties growing up. What would you say was the best thing about your childhood?"

"Finished chores, dinner, and bedtime."

"Where did you go to school for grade nine?"

"My parents sent me to St. John's College, which was an educational institution for the priesthood, located in Edmonton. I boarded there from September till Christmas and then back to the school from January until the end of June. It was my sisters, who were nuns by then, who wanted me to go there to prepare for the priesthood. They convinced my parents, but it didn't work out for me for several reasons. One was that I didn't want to become a priest and another was a very serious infection which nearly killed me."

"So you were at St. John's for just one year?"

"Yes, and that one year was too much. There was a class system there. Many of the kids who came to study were from the cities and they were sons of professional and business people. I was ignored because I was from the farm and assumed, by them, to be stupid and ignorant. Also, I was French Canadian. The farm boys were all seated in the back where we were largely ignored by the priests. The other students were in the front of the classroom where they had the attention of their teachers. There was a monitor who stood at the back of the room watching over the class, and if anyone talked, there was trouble. Understandably, we were bored. It was like a prison. I think that out of the whole group of 100 only four eventually became priests.

"There was never much to look forward to at St. John's. In the morning, the food that we ate was a bowl of porridge, which wasn't very appetizing, but since there was nothing else to eat, we had to grin and bear it, or should I say, grin and eat it. Food was not plentiful, and I remember one guy who was very greedy. He always made sure that he got much more than his share, so there rarely was enough food for all of us. There is always one in every crowd. He was a bully and had a big mouth, always belittling somebody. That was life in those days, and we were not allowed to complain.

"One day, my hand started to swell up and then my arm did as well. It was so swollen you could only see the tips of my fingers. My hand looked like a boxing glove. It was a major infection, and because we had no antibiotics at that time, I knew I was in trouble. It was May 1940, and I spent three weeks in the hospital for treatment which consisted of surgery, a drain in my hand, and soaking my hand and arm in a tub of very hot water for an hour at a time. This was followed by wrapping my arm in a hot wet wool blanket for another hour. This went on for several days.

"One day, the doctor came into my room, with students from the medical school, to examine my arm. He told them he might have to cut the arm off between my shoulder and elbow. By then, I had such a high fever that I was resigned to whatever treatment was required for me to survive. That same day, I could hear a radio playing in a room down the hall. There were six of us in my hospital ward. We strained to hear the report on the radio of the German invasion of France. If I were not in the hospital, I would have been at the college where there was no news. On that day, my life changed forever. I contemplated what my life might become if I survived this horrible infection with my body intact. I decided to enlist in the RCAF. One step toward escape from the farm. I had one visitor while I was in the hospital. He was the priest who gave me the last rites."

"You are telling me that 77 years ago, you were given last rites."

"Yes, and I'm still here. Shortly afterwards, the worst of my illness was over, and there was no amputation. It was time to write my grade nine provincial exams. I hadn't been able to study much because of my illness but I managed to pass with C-."

"I'm not surprised you passed."

"Well, I was!"

"Did you have any fun at all when you were at St. John's?"

"No."

"Do you feel you learned anything there?"

"The only thing I learned was that I certainly didn't want to be a priest! I was still sick after the exams so I went home to recover, go to high school and to work on the farm, until I was able to plan my escape. In the following November, after I started grade ten, my father and my older brother went to a lumber camp, about 50 miles northwest of Bonnyville, to work in the sawmill cutting and piling lumber. My father wanted the materials to build a new barn, a chicken coup, and a garage. There was the 'keeping up with the Joneses' phenomenon going on in our community, and Dad wanted to have the biggest and tallest barn. He pulled me out of school to look after the farm, milking all the cows and caring for 100 head of cattle and 24 horses daily. I worked from 6 a.m. until 10 p.m., fulfilling my duties until Dad got injured in the lumber camp and returned home. Then, I had to replace him at the camp. I found myself cutting lumber by hand in minus 40°F temperatures with a crosscut saw. Even in those temperatures that could freeze our faces, we still had to work.

"That was the end of my high school education."

Chapter 8

'Strength doesn't come from what you can do.
It comes from overcoming the things
you once thought you couldn't do.'
– Anonymous

"There were three other airmen from my community that enrolled the same day as I did, and we were all sent to Brandon, Manitoba, for boot camp. One of the three was a school friend who lived one and a half miles from me, but I never saw him again after boot camp and often wondered what happened to him and if he had survived the war.

"What I thought was a simple act of learning to march and carry a gun, seemed to be a challenge for many of the recruits. The city guys made fun of the farmers. I was frequently admonished to stand up straight because I marched with a lean, the result of a childhood injury. However, after a few days of marching and rifle drills, I was designated to be the marker. Left, right, left turn, right turn, stand at ease, march, halt, about turn. We followed directions mindlessly. It reminded me somewhat of my eight horses following my directions as we plowed, mowed, and raked the fields. Many of the recruits found the guns we carried very heavy and awkward to maneuver, but because I'd spent years developing my muscles by pitching hay and stooking grain, it came naturally to me.

We learned to take orders and keep one's thoughts to oneself, behaviors that I had already spent years learning to acquire.

"After a month or so in boot camp, we were sent home on leave for a month before being sent to Paulson near Dauphin, Manitoba. We spent two months there literally lost. The file for our group somehow got lost, so until it was found again, we were more or less in limbo, not knowing what was going to happen next. Most of our time was spent doing drills and learning and practicing how to load ammunition. Our boredom was occasionally broken by flying. We were at a bombing and gunnery school, so I was able to fly in training activities, sitting beside the pilot and acting as co-pilot. Some of the flying maneuvers were quite scary as we practiced tight turns and simulated dogfights. Occasionally, I had to cope with the centrifugal force. On my first flight, which was over Lake Winnipeg, I wondered if I would ever be able to feel at ease while flying. My apprehension diminished somewhat in the larger planes, but I still was not comfortable. Unfortunately, there were a few crashes, and the new pilots had to become experienced very quickly. We all needed more experience. Eventually, our file was found and we were relocated, after enduring a total of four months of the tedium of boot camp."

"It seems like it was all business getting you guys ready to go into combat."

"They kept us in line so that we were ready for all the lectures and training that lay ahead. With each step in my training, I was getting closer to combat duty in Europe. Suddenly, I was on my way to Montreal. It was a challenging prospect to head off to McGill University to upgrade my grade nine education, the next phase of my training. I found myself among recruits who were also there for officer training too, but who already had grade 13 diplomas or a year of university. For two months, I worked on geometry as well as algebra and English. I struggled with math but found English easy, although it was my second language. As part of the English course exam, I had to write a composition about life on the farm, which I easily accomplished. After writing the exams, the instructor read out the names of the students and their scores, ranked from the lowest to the highest. I thought I had failed because he didn't say my name or my marks. Finally, with a dramatic flourish he read my name at last. My score was in the high 90s. The instructor informed the other students that I was the only French-Canadian in the group, yet now I was at the top of the English class. Having barely passed grade nine with a score of C minus, I was stunned. If anyone had asked me how I felt then, I wouldn't have been able to say a word. I was too astonished to speak."

"You may not have had a much of formal education, but you learned a great deal just by working on the farm."

"I had very little self-confidence when I embarked on my new career."

"So getting high marks at McGill must have indicated to you, that you have a great capacity for learning."

"It helped, but it was still hard to overcome feelings of inadequacy, after hearing degrading comments about me for most of my life. I had done well at McGill. The courses I took, in theory, gave me my senior matriculation. It was quite an education in a relatively short period of time. However, through all of this, my passing mark in Morse code was 65/100 from McGill, not much of an improvement over my earlier scores."

"But it seems to me it's what you learn after your formal education and what you do with your life that counts in the long term."

***Completed Officer's Course, McGill, Montreal, Quebec
February/March 1943***

"That realization came to me much later. I was still at McGill when the Easter holiday arrived and I had a break of four days from my courses. My uncle worked in the maintenance shop for the CPR in Montreal, which required him to commute to and from his home in Quebec City. He invited me to go home with him by train for the Easter weekend, which I happily did. I met my cousin for the first time. He was a few years older than me. His girlfriend had a younger sister who was 18. She had a really beautiful smile. She also was a good Catholic girl. For an adventure, we went to a maple sugar bush out in the country, where they made maple syrup. We rode on a sleigh together behind a horse. On our farm, we had large, very strong horses but this one was a tiny horse that could hardly pull the sleigh. The snow at times was very deep, and the poor horse had a lot of trouble maneuvering through it. I didn't comment on the horse or its struggling, but we spent most of our journey walking behind the sleigh. It was all very nice, although there was no deep intimacy, just holding hands and a few kisses. I was learning that it was very easy to meet girls while I was in the Air Force. I had my girlfriend at home but when I was traveling I met quite a few young ladies."

"So it was similar to a sailor having a lady in each port."

"Right. It was like that for most of my time in the service. When I left the RCAF and I returned home by ship to New York, I phoned my cousin and I would have gone there and married that girl, had the circumstances been different. When we left the service, we were told to go home, get a medical examination, and then get married right away. I think their intention was to put everyone in total misery!

"When I was finished at McGill, I moved further east to Quebec City for six weeks of Ground School where we trained in machine gun operation tactics and aircraft recognition. We had to learn to recognize 265 different planes from any angle. I didn't have any problem with that. But I just could not master Morse code. I didn't have an ear for it. I was also taking more English courses. That part of my training was much more enjoyable.

"My aunt and uncle lived a ten-minute walk from where we were stationed, so they helped alleviate my loneliness. My love of desserts didn't go unnoticed by my aunt, and she made me many treats. She also had a great sense of fun and loved to trick me with a teacup that had a hole in it which allowed tea to drip down my shirt when I drank from it. On another occasion, I was given a bowl of maple syrup and a spoon with a hinge that dripped maple syrup inside my shirtsleeve.

"The next location for our training was Mont Joli, which was 200 miles further east of Quebec City, where we went to

Bombing and Gunnery School. I also spent time in OTS (Officer Training School), where I earned my Sergeant stripes. I also learned how to clean and oil the 200 parts in my machine guns."

"That was a very short time in which you earned your Sergeant stripes."

"Yes. We were there just six weeks. In flying school we didn't really know what flying was all about because we had been instructed on the ground. Now, we were to learn by doing it. Donning a flying suit, we boarded a plane, and the pilot took off. We more or less had to figure out our procedures for ourselves. Because I was familiar with learning how to do things on the farm without instruction, what we had to learn about flying was not that difficult.

"When I arrived in Mont Joli, I met two boys from England. We were sitting together with some other recruits when one of the Englishmen said to the others, 'What is this sleazy Frenchman doing in this course?' I didn't respond to this guy's provocative statement, I just let it go. Later on, we were preparing for our first flight by entering the plane through a small opening in the floor just behind the pilot's seat. It was the escape hatch, for exiting in case we crashed and had to get out. If the plane landed on its belly during a crash, that would have been a big problem. As we were preparing to fly, the kid from England went into the turret where he was supposed to fit the machine gun belt with 303 bullets into. He soon realized he had no idea how to load the required hundreds of bullets. The poor guy had blanched white and was shaking like a leaf. I made my way to him and showed him how to get the guns ready to fire. He was a kid from the city who had never done anything like that before. After receiving my help, he was very nice to me and never again called me degrading names.

"Having worked on the farm for 13 years, I learned very early on, a sense of responsibility. I didn't find it difficult training for action. In fact, I relished the activities but I couldn't imagine what it was like for someone who had never worked before."

"You were training in very close quarters with the guys you flew with and your lives depended on each one properly fulfilling his particular responsibilities."

"I was happy to help anyone. That was how I was raised. Most of the guys did well in theory, but not in practical applications, like handling machine guns. I soon realized that it had been a privilege to be raised in Alberta with a mix of English and French. It made it easy for me to be in the Air Force. Except for my struggle with Morse code! I think I was successful in the war because of what I learned on the farm: to observe and listen. Although I didn't realize it at the time, I gained strength, coordination, stamina, and the ability to work with others under many different circumstances.

The Drogue

"We got into mock battles in training to get ready for the invasion of France. The training had to mimic possible encounters in minute detail, so we could learn the most effective way to engage and take out the enemy. The planes we used to drag a drogue behind were British-made lightweight single engine bombers called 'Ferrey Battles.' The 'drogue' (which looked like a windsock) was attached with a wire and trailed one 150 yards behind, ready for training. We flew our plane parallel to the other manned plane so that the drogue was located behind us where we could practice shooting at it. These mock battles were conducted over the St. Lawrence River. We were given bullets to fire that had been dipped in different paint colors in order to identify the shooter. Each bullet we shot left a colored mark on the drogue. My ammunition was easily identified because my bullets always landed in more or less the same place, on target. Not so with everyone.

"Because of all this training, being fearful of the enemy did not occur to me and no enemy ever surprised me. When a plane approached us from behind, I would prepare to fire at the enemy fighter plane. In reality, not one enemy plane had a chance to open fire on us in 39 missions. If they were too far away for me to shoot them, I would give the pilot instructions for evasive action. Their guns were more powerful than ours, they could shoot at us before they came into the range of our guns. But when the enemy was within range, I used my guns with deadly effect. After graduating my rear gunner training, and before leaving for Europe, I received my badge and Sergeant stripes.

"Before heading off to Halifax to prepare for the trip overseas, I was given a two-week embarkation leave. I boarded the train in Mont Joli and set out on a journey home that would take five days to Bonnyville, Alberta. It was a very slow trip, as the train stopped at every town to pick up milk cans for delivery to the creameries. I guess that's where the term 'the milk run' comes from. I really enjoyed train travel; and like other adventures, it was a chance to meet young ladies. Five days after departure, I arrived home in Bonneville where I hardly slept all weekend. It was a short visit, just four days, and I wanted to visit everyone. Without knowing whether I would ever see my family again, I boarded the train and started my journey to Halifax, from where the new aircrew graduates shipped out to England.

"On the trip east, the seats could be converted to beds, so I got caught up on my sleep between Edmonton and Montreal. Arriving there in the morning, I had to wait all day for the night train to Quebec City. I got off the train thinking I would be spending a boring day in Montreal but luckily I met a nice young lady, with whom I spent the afternoon. We walked up the hill to Mount Royal and then back down to the train station where she waited with me until I left. I never saw her again.

"I called my cousin when I arrived in Quebec City and asked him to meet me at the train station for a quick visit, as I was only making a brief stop. When my cousin came and picked me up, he coerced me into staying for a while. Easily convinced, I spent the next two days with him and also time with the young lady I had met previously. However, the attraction to her was not the same with me as it was before. My aunt and uncle had a cottage at a lake. We went there for the weekend which I should not have done because my leave was going to be finished before I got to Halifax. I would be two days late arriving. To provide me with an excuse, my cousin obtained a letter from a doctor saying I had a gastric problem and could not travel. I'm not a very good liar, so it didn't take Sgt. Maj. Murray long to figure out what had happened. He raked me over the coals for about five minutes, but that was it for punishment. I didn't say a word, which was probably a good thing.

"I think going AWOL for two days was my first real act of rebellion."

Graduation to Sargeant & Air Gunner Wing Presentation,
Mont-Joli, Quebec, July 23rd, 1943

Air Force ID given
on the day Marcel
enlisted

Chapter 9

'Farming is a profession of hope.'
– Anonymous

"One of my sisters who had moved to California to become a nun six years previously finally came home on a holiday. At the time, some of my siblings and I had the measles. It was August, and our bedroom was in the peak of the roof, a very hot place to be. A blanket was arranged over the window to keep the bedroom dark and the light from shining in our eyes and causing us a great deal of pain. We thought we would go blind if the light was not obstructed as we clawed at our itchy rashes. I was burning up with a high fever. Lying in bed on my straw mattress I felt so hot I thought I was going to set it on fire.

"In the heat of that August visit, my sister saddled our old horse named Old Blue to cool off. She used to ride on him to herd the cows home when she was a young girl so she was very familiar with Old Blue. She saddled him up and rode to the back pasture in an area behind the trees so that people wouldn't see her as they passed by on the road. She raced back and forth across the pasture with the fabric of her habit flapping in the wind behind her, resembling a giant crow in flight. It was so nice to have her home. She had been gone six years."

"It sounds like in spite of being so sick, you did not lose your sense of humor. Who did the work when you all were sick?"

"I don't remember. I was too sick to care."

*****

The Croteau Family 1946

"A few years later, in 1932, on a late grey afternoon near the end of November, I had to stay after school because once again I had not completed the previous day's homework assignment. The other members of the family had left with the horse and cutter, leaving me behind to face the consequences. That meant I had to make my own way home. By the time I was ready to go home, the daylight had all but disappeared, leaving me a decision to make…which way should I go? The long way by the road, or the shortcut through the forest, then on to the pasture by the lake on our northern quarter of the farm and then across more open fields. I chose the shorter route through the forest even though I was very fearful of the

79

presence of wolves. When you're a little tot, the thought of wolves being nearby was terrifying. At a very young age, I had a close encounter with a lynx, an event not easily forgotten as it lingered on the edge of consciousness, increasing my fear. Therefore, being wary and having a plan for escape was natural for me. So after walking a hundred yards up the road, I summoned all the courage I could and entered the forest to my right and traveled southwest.

"To protect myself, I chose a sturdy looking stick which also gave me a sense of connection to the forest, a companion, and an extension of myself. I could always bang it on the bushes in case of danger to scare off the unknown creatures and give me time to climb up a tree. I always had one spotted to climb into should I need it for protection. I crossed the creek bed and climbed the opposite bank where I spotted a fresh wolf track in the snow. A shiver of fear ran up my spine. I felt small and helpless as I looked around. I remembered a neighbor telling my father the day before that he had come upon a pair of wolves feeding on a carcass. Trying to put that thought out of my mind, I carried on a few more yards only to find a larger track, likely that of a male. Wolves frequently travel in pairs. The blood rushed through my head, as I thought of all the possibilities, trying to keep calm and to refrain from running away from the danger. Cautiously looking around, I noticed that there were no fresh deer tracks, indicating that the deer that had been in the vicinity had hightailed it off to some other area, a behavior they exhibit when sensing danger, a feeling I myself was experiencing. I was certainly not wanting to hang around either, getting quite anxious knowing another 15 minutes of walking would be necessary to take me out of the forest. In the open, I knew I would feel much safer. Until then, the dark spots that in reality were stumps, seemed to come alive and move. This terrified me as I tried to control my panic and the overwhelming urge to run.

"Upon emerging from the forest, I walked toward the lake by going around some large bushy bluffs. The lake was about one hundred fifty yards to my right. By this time my stick and I were one, sharing the same energy. Approaching the lake on my immediate right, I looked up to see up a huge grey wolf staring at me as he sat on his haunches. Even in the darkness, I could see his piercing eyes, although I was about 100 yards away. My heart was pounding in my chest, my stomach tightened. I felt faint as I tightened the grip on my stick. I panicked and started running as fast as I could, my legs going like windmills, my mind racing. I thought of a thousand things, mainly wishing my dog at the time, named Sport, was with me. He was not as big as a wolf but was not afraid of anything. Instinctively, I hollered, 'Sport,' as that is how we called out to him. As I quickly glanced around me, the wolf came running after me. He was not far behind and closing in. I sped up, dropping my stick which fell between my legs and tripped me causing me to land on my back sending the snow flying. As the wolf jumped on me, my mind went into no time or space, a continuum of atonement. I closed my eyes and waited for my flesh to be torn to shreds. Suddenly, I felt something warm licking my face. I opened my eyes… Sport always showed up when he was called!

I was nine years old."

*****

"I gather you were not close to your older brother nor your younger one and didn't spend much time with them. In

what little spare time you enjoyed, what did you do to amuse yourself?"

"My father knew I trained horses, but when he was not around, I took two one and a half year old oxen (neutered bulls) and tried to train them. I knew it would not be easy. When my father bought his first acreage, which was forested, he could not afford horses. Instead, he bought a plow and two oxen to help him clear the land. They were not particularly cooperative. When they didn't want to work anymore, they would slump down to the ground and remain there with a blank but stubborn look on their faces. You could poke them with a stick, and they would not budge. They responded to nothing unless it inflicted a sharp pain. Our dog had to be engaged to nip at them which he did, prompting the oxen to continue with their task. Armed with this information, I knew they wouldn't like being told what to do so I carried a thin branch which I waived around.

"My dog Barney was a big asset to my training procedures. He knew what I needed and nipped the backs of their legs. That got their attention! They were not very intelligent animals, but after a lot of repetitive instruction, eventually they understood what I wanted and they obeyed. Their cooperation allowed me to hitch them up together. We had a sleigh that was constructed with planks seven feet long and about 18 inches wide attached to runners. The platform was all made from birch and was bolted together, thus giving me a sturdy platform on which to ride while the oxen pulled me. I dared not damage the sleigh or I would be in deep trouble. I coaxed these animals onto the road with the stick and then signaled them to start running until they ran out of wind. I was able to stop them as they soon started to learn the lines and obey my commands. Before long, they were working as a team to pull the sleigh. I did all of this when nobody was around.

"One day, our neighbor, who must've been about 15 years older than my father and who was quite a gentleman, came to our home. It was Election Day, and he picked up my dad with his horse and cutter to go to vote. Nearby, I was hiding behind some bushes so I could check my little steers to make sure they were ready for my plan. My dad and our neighbor were busy talking while the horse walked along the road taking them to their destination. I signaled to my oxen, which were pulling my sleigh, to run at full speed. We caught up with my dad and his friend and raced past them on the road."

"I would love to have seen the look on your father's face as you sped by!"

"The horse was startled by the racing oxen and ran off the road toward the edge of the ditch which ran the length of the road. They almost turned over as the cutter swayed seemingly out of control behind the horse. My father yelled at me, 'Go home! Get out of here!' My father never said anything nice to me and he certainly wasn't going to start now. He was mad at me for behaving like this in front of his friend and terrifying the poor horse with all the noise created by the oxen running past. I suspect if it had been one of my brothers who had done this, my father would not have been so angry. What I had done was such a surprise to him. I rarely shared with my father what was going on in my life because he never seemed to approve of anything I did."

"So after your dad found out what you were doing, were you ever able to race with your oxen again?"

"Well, I more or less lost interest because spring was coming and that meant more work and less free time. Besides,

I spent a year or two training the steers and had accomplished what I set out to do."

*****

"I loved working with animals and training them because they were not judgmental and for the most part were eager to please. My dog Barney, who replaced Sport after his death, was a perfect example, and we became best friends. Our many adventures together only strengthened the bond we had. Whenever we had any spare time after completing our chores, my siblings and I would search out a way to create our own fun either together or for me, more often alone.

"Our family had one pair of skates which had been sent to us along with a trunk of clothes from relatives in Quebec. Their family was about 10 or 15 years older than ours. The skates apparently were for goalies because the blades were not worn down. Depending on who was wearing the skates, we stuffed them with old felt boots and then filled the toes with enough paper to make the boot fit. We tied them on, wrapping twine around the ankles, and then went for a skate across the pond or lake. Because we had to share one pair, none of us ever got much ice time except for my older brother who managed to get as much time as he wanted. I wanted to play hockey when I was 14 or 15 but could not because we lived too far from town and I had no skates of my own. To my father's credit, he offered to buy me skates as payment for stooking a field of grain. I was so keen to acquire those skates that I took my dog out to the field and arranged the bundles of grain into stooks late into the night, working by moonlight. My brother emerged from his usual hiding place in the barn just in time to help me finish stooking the field. Dad showed up just as we were finishing and heard my brother announce: 'Hey, Dad, look what I did.' My father never did buy me skates. One more promise that was made but never fulfilled.

"When I was 17, my mother bought me a pair of skates for $2.98 which would eventually get passed down to my younger siblings. The train brought the mail to Bonnyville three times a week arriving at 7:30 p.m. The mail was then taken to the post office to be sorted. The post office was opened at nine o'clock at night for the mail to be picked up by the residents. In the winter, the cars were always driven tentatively on the icy roads as the drivers made their way to the post office. They often had bald tires. It was the end of the depression and many still could not afford new tires.

"My dog Barney was full of energy and loved to chase cars. In preparation for some fun, I laced my skates up, and my dog had his collar on while we patiently waited by the side of the icy road. When a car approached, I would grab Barney's collar with him positioned between my legs while we prepared for takeoff. As the car went by us, my dog leaped into action to race alongside, trying to bite the tires. I crouched behind him holding onto his collar while he pulled me along the icy road. A few times he went so fast, he would get a cramp in the back of one of his legs. He continued down the road, running on three legs. I stopped him and rubbed his leg to release the cramping and then let him start running again but very slowly. Thankfully, this didn't happen very often during our skating escapades. I'm sure that whoever was in the car could hear him barking as he ran alongside the car, but I'm not so sure they knew I was flying along behind him."

****

"Although I had been taken out of Grade ten to work on the farm, I hosted a winter party in January for my former classmates at my home. There were both guys and gals who planned to attend. Therefore, I wanted to create a good impression. I thought perhaps some rodeo antics might do just that.

"In preparation for my tricks, I harnessed two of our horses, one a purebred race horse and the other one a Clydesdale cross, to a sleigh that was attached in two parts. It was used for hauling grain but could easily accommodate my guests.

"After my friends arrived, we walked to the barn where I proceeded to seat all of them on the sleigh to take them for a ride. When we were ready, including the horses, I mounted one of them and stood on its back. I put my cowboy hat on my head and signaled for the horses to take off. We raced along at what seemed like 30 miles per hour, while I jumped from one horse to the other, all the while tossing my hat in the air and catching it.

"For my next trick, I laid a hat, then a scarf, and then a knife some distance apart on the ground. I mounted our racehorse and at full speed I raced toward the items, picking up each one while using my ankle and foot hooked around the horn of my saddle to keep me from falling off my horse to the ground. The horse was running so fast, I thought he was going to run right into the side of the barn. When we finally came to a stop, I asked if anyone wanted to duplicate my hijinks but I had no takers."

Chapter 10

'Men and women whose early life was shaped in the ordeal
of the Great Depression showed the values formed in that
crucible when tyranny threatened the world.'

– Steve Buyer

*"You worked very hard when you were a child. Did your
family ever take time to celebrate special occasions, especially
important dates like birthdays or Christmas?"*

"We rarely celebrated birthdays but we were Catholics so
we acknowledged and celebrated Christmas. In 1929, the
Depression had started and there was very little cash and none
for gifts. My mother had to be creative. Therefore, throughout
the year, she bought big bars of PG White Laundry Soap for
washing our clothes and for washing our hands.

My mother clipped and collected the coupons from the soapboxes. When she had enough of them to redeem for gifts, she mailed them to the Proctor and Gamble Company. One year she sent them in return for Christmas presents: a toy car for my brother and a little doll for my younger sister. I got nothing. Previously, I had been given three or four gifts: a train set, a little car, and I'm not sure I can remember what else. The last time I was given gifts, I was five or six. After that, I was too old for presents.

"The local car dealer came to my dad's farm in 1929, on a Sunday. He wanted to sell Dad a new car and offered to take a certain amount of wheat as payment. Although we did not have a car at the time, my dad said he'd think about it. The very next day, wheat fell in price from $1.50 to $0.12 a bushel. I'm sure the car dealer was happy the deal was not finalized."

"How did your father react? Was he upset at not having followed through with the barter?"

"As was his custom, he said nothing."

"Was the Depression less difficult for you because your family was quite self-sufficient then, including growing your own food?"

"When I came back from the war, I thought I should go farming because of my experience during the Depression when we regularly encountered folks begging at our door for food. I learned then that living on the farm could protect us from all kinds of difficulties in life.

"In those days, there were no fresh vegetables in the market, so my mother would spend all summer canning our home grown produce. We grew lots of root vegetables: turnips, potatoes, carrots, and parsnips which we stored in a small root cellar which was basically a hole with a door in a large mound of dirt.

"It was such a different time. Our lifestyle then did not resemble society now. Our spirit was quite different from the pioneer days around the turn of the 20th century. Then, people at least had a sense of hope for a better future. After all, could things get any worse? And then came along the Great Depression. There was so much hopelessness, and everyone had empty pockets. The banks closed only to re-open sometime later with a new name. Meanwhile, the bank customers had lost their savings and were reluctant to use banks again. It seemed like a huge darkness had settled over us. There was very little work in the cities, and many people were almost starving.

"Mr. Bennett was prime minister from 1930 to 1935. Many who had been well heeled enough to have cars were unfortunately unable to afford gas. To handle their transportation needs, the transmission and motor were taken out of the car to reduce the weight. The windshield was removed so that horses could be harnessed to the front of the car. They called them Bennett buggies, and one could observe many of them on the streets. I remember my Uncle had an Auckland car and he loved to race past our house with his fast team of horses pulling his car. I think that's where the term 'horsepower' came from! Cars with their air-filled tires made traveling much more comfortable than riding in a buggy. Another consequence of the Depression was that many car manufacturers went out of business for lack of sales. Many other businesses struggled and failed too.

The Bennett Buggy

"There was an old storekeeper whose name was Houlihan whose shop I passed every day on my way to school. We learned he was an Irish/Frenchman. He came to Bonnyville from Quebec where he had been living after immigrating to Canada from Ireland. In those days, if you lived in Quebec, you had to speak French. It was the first store in our community and not much of one at that. The building was quite old, probably one of the earliest built. It had never been painted and the siding was all curled up from sun damage and cold winters. The family lived upstairs. People thought the old man didn't like to spend money but more likely he just didn't have any.

"Mr. Houlihan's idea of running a store might not have been conventional but he did try to meet his customer's needs. He made a bench from willow branches which he positioned on the porch of his store to provide some seating for his customers. Also, there was always a 100-pound bag of flour with a discounted price to be found on the porch. He had his merchandise arranged so that people could easily see his limited stock as they entered the store.

"The first owner of the store was named McLeod and he had the local telegraph service inside his store. One of my aunts worked for him when she was young; and because she knew Morse code, she operated the telegraph. Eventually, telephone service came to Bonnyville, but it took a while before everyone acquired one of those newfangled communication devices. In the meantime, if you wanted to telephone someone, you went to the store to make your call. Mr. McLeod asked the operator to record the length of the call so that he could charge accordingly for the use of the phone.

"One day on my way to school, I was walking along a dirt road and I saw a penny lying at my feet. I picked up the coin and realized it was a rusty nickel. When we were kids, we never had a penny or a nickel, much less a dime. Even though I would have preferred a dime, I felt rich!"

"That was your lucky day."

"Yes, and I could not wait to spend it. I had to scratch the rust off of my nickel in order to present it to the old storekeeper. When he looked at it, he insisted it was just a penny, so I took it home and polished it till it sparkled. He finally accepted it. I bought two chocolate bars, but they were probably five years old."

"I guess he didn't have a big turnover of merchandise."

"No, he sure didn't. He kept a glass container on the counter in which he stored Christmas candy year round. I remember when my kid brother started school, he was just five, and the school was situated on a hill two and three quarters of a mile from home. He liked to stop at the store on his way to school. One day, temptation overcame him and he reached over the counter and took one of the candies out of the jar. He popped it in his mouth, but the old man saw him do it and told him to take the candy out of his mouth and put it back in the candy jar, which of course he did."

"Oh dear, this is going from stale chocolate bars to worse."

"But that's the way it was. We had to scrutinize our purchases, especially canned goods. We never bought tomatoes or any other canned foods because we didn't know how long they'd been in the store. There were no date stamps in those days. We actually hardly bought anything except flour every now and then, only if we ran out of our own supply. There was a guy from Scotland who was a miller. When he moved to Bonnyville, he built a flourmill. My dad was a customer. When we needed our supplies replenished, he filled our wagon with a load of wheat and drove it to the mill to have bags of flour, cream of wheat, and bran milled for our use. When he returned home with the milled grain, flour was stored in each bedroom, two or three bags in a room. They were stacked on top of each other and a sheet was thrown over them. When Mother made bread, she wanted to add some of the bran into the flour mixture which did not go over well with my father. He was raised in a flourmill in Quebec which made him very particular about the whiteness of the flour. In Quebec, the people who were poor ate whole grain brown bread. The well-to-do ate white bread."

"Well, we've done a bit of a turn around since then regarding white bread. These stories from your past are important because most people today have no idea how it was and what daily life was like in 1929 after the markets crashed and the Great Depression began."

"Dad finally decided in 1930 to buy a car, a 1925 Ford Model T. He purchased it from an old man who never used the car when it rained, or during the winter. Therefore, when my dad acquired it, it was just like new; although, he could have purchased something much more modern for the same amount of money. We drove the Ford model T until 1937 when it was replaced with a 1929 model which was also was just like new with plush seats. We thought it was very luxurious. During the Depression, Dad's car spent a lot of time sitting on blocks in the shed. For two years, he could not afford to license it or repair the timing belt. My father was not very mechanically minded so he could not repair it himself. He also had trouble driving with a clutch. It was always easy to tell who was driving our car as it lurched down the street."

"Could you get your whole family into the car?"

"More or less! The model T was black, and there were two rows of seats in the back. The younger ones sat on the knees of the older siblings as we drove it to church at about five miles an hour. We could almost have walked faster than that. The roads weren't that great in the 30s, so one could not drive recklessly. After the Depression, the economy changed dramatically, and there were more cars and better roads. Gradually, life started to improve in 1936 when the price of grain increased."

"So would wheat have doubled in value during that time?"

"Well, much more. It went to a dollar a bushel from $0.12 a bushel. During the Depression, the banks closed. There was no stability in the economy. As a result, there was no money to be made, so there was no money to hire help. We worked two hours in the morning before going to school and worked again after school, not always having time to finish our homework before bedtime. Nevertheless, we made our contribution to the economy of the family. There were very few farmers who worked the way we did in my family. Not many grain farmers also had a dairy, beef cattle, and pig operation. The children from families that had straight grain farms didn't work the way we did. On our farm, there was always something for us to do."

"So the stories you've told me about mischief making were not everyday occurrences."

"Definitely not. Our main focus at home was trying to get the work done that was required of us. When we were kids, we were judged by our physical prowess and ability to work hard, not our ability to read and write, neither of which my father could do.

"I remember more about events that happened 70 or 80 years ago than I do about what happened yesterday or last week or last month. Perhaps, I spend too much time reminiscing."

"Well, I don't think that is such a bad idea. It's good to be able to reflect on the past, especially when it's an interesting life like yours. Besides, I think it's important to know our history and especially to learn about it from someone who lived it. It's a wonderful gift you are sharing with us."

"I enjoy remembering all the little details. I can remember going to herd the cattle and seeing all the little plants that were growing in the pastures."

"You do seem to have a fantastic visual memory. How lucky am I and others to be the beneficiaries of your storytelling of experiences, insights, and wisdom, the changes you have seen and the way you have adapted to so many situations in your life."

"It's easy to adapt when it's your own life. It's not difficult, you just let it happen. The world is always changing just like the clouds rolling by overhead, each one completely different in shape from a moment ago. I would never have dreamt of the life I have today. I was able to go to art school at 72 in contrast to my grandfather who was still making windows and doors at age 82 to support himself."

*****

"How did the day to day hardships you encountered during your service overseas compare with your experiences during the Depression?"

"I think the depression gave me a good grounding for what I was going to encounter in England. You might say my expectations were rather low. During the war, the shortage of food was a significant day-to-day problem for the enlisted and everyone else. The army recruits received the most calories in a day because they were considered to be more physically active than the air force or the navy. The officers also ate better than the rest of us. Because my squadron flew at night, we frequently missed breakfast upon our return to base in the morning. I got in the habit at dinnertime of slipping a few slices of Canadian cheddar cheese, when it was available, between two pieces of bread and concealing it in my pocket. My sandwich was saved to eat after our mission for the night was finished. Between missions and leaves, we spent our days on call for our next sortie. There was a loudspeaker at the airport which alerted us with the message: 'Attention, attention! The following crews will report to the briefing room.' This was followed by the pilot's name who was later joined by his crew. If our crew were not called, we spent most of the day lying on our cots, catching up on our sleep.

Before leaving on a mission, we went to the mess hall to eat what we all called 'The Last Supper.' This meal was two slices of bacon and two eggs with toast. That was the only time we saw fresh eggs. Most of the time, it was powdered eggs from Canada. Occasionally, we were served Canadian cheddar which was a treat. Usually, our meals were vegetables with very little meat. Meat was rationed because fresh meat could not be imported across the ocean to supplement local supplies. We soon became very tired of that diet. The soup we were served was usually mutton soup consisting mostly of fat. Kidney stew was not much more palatable. Most of the guys had never seen or consumed kidney stew which gave me the opportunity to clean up the leftovers even though I had never eaten kidneys before either. I was that hungry! Coming from the farm, there was never a shortage of food. We always had plenty of fresh vegetables in the summer and canned and root vegetables in the winter along with meat.

"The kindness of the Brits was shown to us in many ways and on many occasions. Sometimes, it was just a kind word of thanks or encouragement, sometimes, it was much more.

"One early morning, after the Normandy invasion and the German Army had stopped the Allies, the Americans were bombing the German troops who were blocking the approach of the Canadian Army. We took off from our base on a bombing mission in the dark but it was light by the time we flew over France. Arriving at our destination, we encountered huge clouds forming a thunderhead right over the target. There were four hundred bombers coming in at 18,000 feet. The master bomber radioed us to get down underneath that storm in order to see the target. Following orders, each plane opened the bomb bays and put the flaps and the wheels down to slow the airplane. All the bombers were coming down like a flock of geese, so close together. Our crew got under the cloud, maybe one third of the way in, but by the time we got to where we were to drop our bombs, others bombs were already exploding down there. We were at 1,000 feet in the midst of the explosions. It was like a machine gun of bombs going off all around us. The aircraft was shaking so intensely the pilot couldn't read his instruments. He tried to re-calibrate after the shocks from the bombs but the airplane was still shaking. Finally we dropped our bombs too. Then everybody went up into the clouds to get out of the way.

"Later, we learned there were eight collisions and eight planes missing. Our pilot kept going up and up into the clouds thinking he would eventually come out on top of the storm. But in doing so, he had burned most of our fuel having opened the motors at full bore. As we started to go home, the engineer informed us that the gas tanks were nearly empty. He knew we would never make it back to base. His solution was to ditch in the ocean. Therefore, down we went to a lower altitude. The channel was covered in clouds, as we desperately looked for an opening so we could see where we wanted to go. Finally, we found a hole through which the pilot flew. We were down below the cloud cover for about 20 minutes approaching the British coastline when we found a British airport right on the coast. Much to the crew's relief, the pilot quickly landed. We were totally out of gas by now and two of our four motors quit working on the runway. But we were able to stop safely and all of us breathed a huge sigh of relief. The good news was that if we had crash-landed there would have been no fire!

"A few minutes before our arrival, an American squadron had taken off for an airport in France. Therefore, there was no fuel left at the airport. A fuel truck was ordered but because of the invasion a few days earlier, it was going to take two days to get fuel before we could fly to home base. Fortunately, the airport was near a resort on the beach. Our flying clothes were left at the airport before we headed to the resort. Our navigator chose to wear his pajamas which created a bit of a stir. There were a lot of tourists, people on leave from the factories and wartime duties. Lots of young ladies were there, asking what kind of crew we were because of our navigator's attire. They had never seen pajamas before, apparently because in England, men wore nightshirts.

"Since there was nothing for us at the vacant airport, we went to find accommodation elsewhere. I met a young lady on the beach, and she took me home to her parents. Thankfully, they agreed to let me sleep there for two nights. They fed me even though they didn't have much for themselves. Breakfast was a just a slice of raisin bread which was toasted, but they were willing to share. For lunch, we went to a restaurant that offered us a rarebit. That was the first time I ever heard that word. I assumed it was rabbit, so hungrily I said, 'I'll have the rabbit, please.' They brought me a piece of toast with a bit of cheese on it!!! Maybe they thought I was joking, but I wasn't. We stayed there for two days, filled our plane with gas when it arrived, and flew back to our base. Our visit there was like a little holiday, a reprieve without a leave pass, although the skipper had informed our base of the situation. It was a really nice break to have the time on the beach. The English were very receptive to Canadians. Our hosts were all on food rations, but they were willing to share with us what little they had. Everybody was involved in the war effort and unselfishly took care of us during our brief visit. The general state of mind in England was quite different than in some parts of Canada. In northern Alberta where I came from, most of the French Canadians and the Church were against going to war. However, those of us who made the decision to join the fight appreciated the hospitality and gratitude of the English for our participation in the war effort."

Chapter 11

'Do not fight with time.
It moves at its own pace.'
– Marcel Croteau

"I had six weeks to wait in Halifax for the Queen Mary, the cruise ship that had been converted into a troop and supply carrier, to take us Britain. No specific training was scheduled during the wait. It was up to the enlisted to figure out how to spend the time. The pay wasn't that great; and since I had recently been on leave, I didn't have much money. Also, I was committed to sending half of my pay home so I didn't have the resources to go out very often. My cohorts were more or less in the same situation.

"During this period, I started drinking too much. One night, there were three of us hanging out in the mess hall where alcoholic beverages were available. We each bought a round of beer, and it was too much for me. I was sitting with the guys with my elbow on the table and my hand under my chin to prop up my head. Naturally, whenever I relaxed, my hand would drop and my head banged on the table. Eventually, my friends walked me back to the barracks to my room on the second floor. I was not used to drinking so getting sick was the consequence. I hung my head and upper body out the window with the guys holding onto my legs so I wouldn't flip out of the room to the ground below. In the morning, the inevitable hangover was an unpleasant reminder of the night before. I never forgot that night when I used alcohol to relieve, at least for a short time, my high anxiety and boredom. Unfortunately, that experience did not influence the choices I was to make later in my life around the use of alcohol.

"My roommate and I used our abundance of free time to check out the city of Halifax. There were no pubs open in Halifax in those days. Perhaps, that was a good thing. We frequently walked down to Halifax Harbor. One day, there were just two of us when we encountered a bunch of sailors at the docks who liked to beat up the 'pigeons,' slang for airmen. Not that I was afraid but I didn't want to get involved in a fight and reinforce the degree of rivalry that already existed between the Air Force and the Navy.

"After all our training in Canada, we were anxious to get on with the job, which was more training in England then, combat. The wait in Halifax for our transport across the Atlantic was excruciatingly boring. I could see the Queen Mary docked there in the harbor, as it waited for troops to come from the United States for transport along with Canadians to Scotland. This was in August 1943. The Queen Mary had the distinction of being the ship that transferred the largest number of troops from North America to Britain in one year of the war. There were 12,500 on board on each trip, so the numbers added up quickly.

"After the war, plaques were displayed inside the Queen Mary, now docked in San Diego. The names of every soldier who travelled on the ship during the war are engraved on those plaques. My name is included in the archives along with thousands of others."

"I saw the Queen Mary in Los Angeles a few years ago and even though I have traveled on some large cruise ships, I can't imagine how they squeezed over 12,000 troops onto that ship. The logistics of accommodating that many people must have been a nightmare!"

"The cabins were altered to accommodate the huge numbers of passengers. Each little cabin had two rows of hammocks stacked three on top of each other so that the person in the top hammock had his nose almost rubbing the ceiling. We spent 24 hours inside the ship and 24 hours on deck. It was August when we traveled, so it was quite beautiful sleeping outside on the deck. We all had a blanket issued to us but that was it. Fortunately, it was nice and warm because it was summer, and we followed the Gulf Stream.

"It took only four days at sea to travel from Halifax to Scotland because the ship was at full bore to reduce exposure to the enemy submarines. To further evade the subs, the Queen Mary was constantly changing course. For the first time in my life, I saw whales and dolphins in the ocean as we passed by, quite an exciting event for a farm boy from Alberta. Those sightings were pleasant moments of distraction for those of us who were heading to war."

"What was the food like?"

"It was mash. Everything was put through a grinder of some kind. It was quickly slopped by spoon onto metal mess plates. We had to run through the line because there were so many people to feed at each meal. They gave us a spoon to eat with which helped speed up the process given the fact that the food didn't need chewing. There was no eating leisurely with mindfulness as we rushed to finish in order to accommodate the feeding of 12,500 people, giving a new meaning to feeding a crowd of 5,000 with the loaves and fishes. It felt like being on an assembly line in a factory.

The Queen Mary

"In spite of the crowded conditions, the trip across the Atlantic was enjoyable and memorable. We managed to arrive safely. After docking in Greenoch, Scotland, we remained on board for two days. It took that long to unload the troops and supplies. Fortunately, the tuck shop was resupplied so that one could buy a carton of cigarettes which was sold for $2.35. There was no tax so that was a bonus. We also had to wait for the trains that would take us to our training destinations in England."

Chapter 12

'There is nothing like a target
to improve your aim.'
– Aristotle

"Before I enlisted, I had never been anywhere except to the village of Bonnyville so it was quite a new experience to land in Grenoch, Scotland, a city made of stone and with a sky filled with chimneys. I was anxious to get off the ship and to start exploring. However, there was a wait to disembark the supplies and the troops that sailed from Halifax. The delay cut into my time to look around the town. From Grenoch, we boarded a ferry which took us to Glasgow. All we had with us was a duffel bag and a kit bag which contained our personal items. Our anticipation of more training and then action made the wait very boring during the few days it took for the trains to arrive to take us to the next destination, Bournemouth. Luckily for us, Bournemouth, a tourist destination, was located on the south coast of England, on the shores of the English Channel. It was the end of August when we arrived and all the hotels had been converted to barracks. Again, we had a leisurely wait of three weeks, passing our days on the beach, watching the girls. All of that was about to change.

"Before we started our intensive training, we were taken to London to observe first-hand how the bombing of the city had deeply affected the residents. The physical damage to the city was almost surreal. I have images burned into my memory of visiting the Underground stations where many victims, bombed out of their homes, had taken up residence. Mattresses and personal belongings were lined up against the walls next to the train tracks. During the day, there were guards watching over these makeshift homes to prevent theft while the inhabitants were at work. I will never forget the haunted, desperate looks of despair I saw on the faces of those Londoners forced into this nightmare.

"It was also shocking when during training we flew over the city of Sheffield which had been bombed by the Luftewaffe. Only a few partially bombed buildings were left standing in the flattened industrial city. The purpose, of course, of these trips was to intensify our resolve to fight the enemy.

"Our next destination was the Air Force base about eight miles from Pershore in Worcestershire, England, where we were to form crews but the wait there was not going to be leisurely. Immediately, we were assigned the task of breaking up rocks for landscaping the site. The English officers treated us like slaves, but we got the crushed stone laid around the sidewalks in short order. Thus, we acquired another skill we did not previously have!

"Finally, we were 'crewed up.' My assigned group was comprised of French Canadians including two guys that I already knew because we had crossed the Atlantic together. One was a wireless operator from Fort William (now Thunder Bay, Ontario) with whom I connected more easily than most of the others who were Quebecois and who seemed to me like they were from another country. I was a farm boy, and they were from the city. Another was a guy named Gagnon with whom I had gone to the Catholic College. The husband of one of my teachers and who was a school inspector was there too. He was a very nice man, 42 years old and was 'crewed up' with all officers. He had been the chief recruiting officer in Montreal. In order to enlist as an air gunner, he had to be demoted. Actually, I was quite impressed with him but wondered if his motivation to join up at his age might have been to get away from his wife, who was a teacher I didn't particularly like. She disciplined us with a steel-edged ruler."

"Was that a good thing that you met up with some people you knew? Did you feel more comfortable and less lonely?"

"Yes. It was interesting to get to know them more. We all tried to keep busy, which meant trying to get to know lots of strangers. For the most part, it was a comfortable situation because most of the guys were usually inclusive. After all, we were brought together for a noble cause. However, we occasionally encountered the pettiness, jealousies, and narrow-mindedness that can be evident in any group in society. It was important for each member of a crew to remain together throughout one's service in order to learn as much as possible about each individual's techniques used to perform his job. So we had to get along. That meant setting any differences aside, not always easily done, but necessary to create a well-oiled machine where everyone could anticipate each other's actions.

"While we were waiting for crew formation, we engaged in some fairly basic flight training. The first time I went up in a Wellington bomber there were two gunners assigned, myself, and the school inspector. It was also the first time we were going to participate in air-to-air firing. He went ahead of me into the turret and immediately came back out, looking very old and white as a sheet. The poor guy was claustrophobic. That was the only time I crewed with him. He was an officer so he ate in the officer's mess and crewed with other officers.

I lost track of him. Then, only a week after we started training, he and his crew crashed and they were all killed.

"On some of the training flights, I was able to learn how to operate my machine guns. It was not difficult, and I soon learned to fire with both hands. I had four machine guns. Each one shot 4,200 rounds a minute or 74 rounds a second. If the enemy ever got close enough, they were shot out of the air before they knew what hit them. We had live ammunition for practice, and I learned how to sit there in the confined space of the turret and fire accurately."

"What did you do to alleviate all the stress I would think you were feeling regarding the training you were undertaking and already the loss of some friends?"

"At the time, I had to learn to compartmentalize our actions in order to be able to separate one's self from the awfulness we were engaged in. It was the only way to cope. The repercussions would surface later.

"We also had to find ways to distract ourselves from the weight of our actions. Once we had finished our training for the day, if we were not too exhausted, my buddies and I would search out some fun. Our base at Pershore was about four miles from the town. There was no transportation, so we walked there to an amusement park where among other things we could meet girls. We were as excited as kids with the prospect of having some fun and a change of pace. We often ended the evening by walking the ladies home."

"How often did you go there?"

"I went as often as I could get away. There was always someone to go with. It was all new to me, offering me activities I had never done before. In some ways, though, our farm was like an amusement park. We had three saddle horses and usually a total of 24 horses depending on how many foals were born in the spring. However, there was nothing mechanical like tractors on the farm, just the horses that we worked with. So all these new mechanical rides were fascinating to me. I was just like a little boy!

Wellington Bombers , used as long range bombers in the early years of the war over Europe and North Africa were retired from combat and used for operational training on which Croteau and Crew completed their operational training at Stratford on Avon , England.

"My crew was an interesting bunch of guys with whom I would spend the rest of my flying time. We were the 'Alouettes,' all chosen because we were French Canadians and therefore deemed to have a lot in common. Which just goes to show how little knowledge most people had about the French in Canada. Even our language has a lot of differences. None of my cohorts were farmers, so I felt like the odd man out. I had much to learn about them, and they had a lot to learn about me."

"Raised in the city, they would have had a much different experience than you had growing up in Northern Alberta."

"Yes, I was totally different, so they called me 'the cowboy.' And I guess that's really what I was. Our horses and cattle needed tending to and that's how I worked every morning till night. We rode the horses to herd the cattle. We milked cows and performed whatever chores needed to be done, depending on who got there first. There was always something to do.

"I better get back to the war. It's much heavier stuff and it's hard to talk about."

"I think it's good to take a break to remember some of the ways you managed to distract yourself from the gut-wrenching situations you experienced."

"In order to be as highly skilled as possible, more training was required. So from Pershore where we were 'crewed' up, our final training was to be at an airbase at Stratford-upon-Avon. There we flew Wellingtons for our night training so that the conditions would be the same when we went into action. The Wellington was generally flown at about 18,000 feet which was a comfortable altitude for it. Our training route was a circle that took us up over Scotland and the Shetlands, over the ocean and across Ireland then back to Stratford-upon-Avon. Each training flight usually took five hours and at 18,000 feet with no heat, it was very cold. This was in December when the temperatures were about -20°F in the rear turret so I was chilled to the bone by the time our training flights were done. I recently watched a documentary that was about WWII Bomber Command, and in it, they said that the winter temperature in the rear turret could be as low as -50 to -55°C. When we flew through the clouds in winter in such cold temperatures, there was a serious problem with the icing on the plane. If I talked to the pilot, he was very angry because he did not want me to say a word even though I had a good view from my position in the glassed-in rear turret of what was going on outside. He was busy concentrating on changing altitude in order to get an inversion so the ice would break off the wings. That's how the school inspector and his crew crashed. They had an icing problem they could not fix. It was a very dangerous problem. The ice not only added weight to the plane, but it changed the passage of air over the wings. If the plane's engines stopped from icing, right away you lost the air stream that kept the plane suspended in the air. I found myself in the back of the airplane watching all this and not being allowed say a word."

"You certainly experienced some serious hazards, coping with those incredibly cold temperatures. How did you keep from freezing?"

"I was born and raised in northern Alberta which is one of the coldest places in Canada. Winter Arctic blasts of weather generally caused our temperatures to drop to anywhere from -30° to -50°C. Therefore, working in frigid temperatures was not new to me."

"I'm curious about the clothing you wore."

"We were issued silk stockings for our feet! I'm not kidding. They were not like ladies stockings but were white and thick and kept the heat in. Over them, we wore heavy wool socks and flying boots that were lined with sheepskin. All those layers helped. We wore heavy quilted coats which we topped with a big canvas-flying suit with lots of pockets. Insulated gloves kept our hands warm but made movement very awkward as did the rest of our clothing. The extreme cold was more of an issue for the rear gunner than the rest of the crew because they had the benefit of heat from the motors and generators. Half way through my service, rear air gunners were given electric suits to wear. They were the forerunners of electric blankets. This meant that we did not have to wear so many layers of clothing. We also had electric boots that snapped onto the suit legs. The concept of the electric suits was great but a few bugs needed to be ironed out. Unfortunately, we had to dress in our suits in the fuselage. Then we walked to get into the turret wearing the boots which could cause a breakage in the wiring which in turn caused an electric short. This was the worst enemy I ever had because my feet would catch on fire and the boots would have to be removed immediately.

"At altitudes of 10,000 feet or more, we also wore oxygen masks. I regularly had to break off the ice that formed on my oxygen tube and my eyebrows kept icing while I was bouncing around in the tail of the plane. It was unnerving. The pilot wasn't interested in my problems, he had enough of his own as did the rest of the crew. He made sharp turns more often than I would have liked but that was because of storms that were interfering with our flight path. All of us had to keep quiet and just sit there and endure.

The Alouette Squadron 425

"It was difficult not being a Quebecois when they all communicated in a version of French that I was not familiar with. We were supposed to repeat all communications in English but it was unusual for us to do so. I needed to quickly learn the French terms I was not familiar with and be very careful. It was like stepping on eggshells all the time. These guys were very critical of each other and especially me. I think trying to hang onto one's culture (which was what I thought they were trying to do) can make one very insecure and difficult. I was not very good at arguing so I let them say what they had to say and I would say nothing."

"Being confrontational does not seem to me to be part of your personality."

"Maybe I had difficulty responding verbally but I could take care of myself physically. Hanging out in the barracks, there was frequently roughhousing going on. We were young men and started physically engaging with one another in an unstructured form of wrestling."

"I can relate to that. I raised three boys and I can remember seeing Dian Fossey's video about her work with gorillas. The young males interacting with each other in play reminded me so much of my sons that I never again tried to stop them from wrestling. I just asked them to go outside before they broke the furniture."

"I think it was a form of stress release or maybe there was just too much testosterone in the room. In one situation, there were five of us. I took them all and piled them one on top of the other. I don't think they liked me very much."

"They found out that you were a force to be reckoned with."

"Years of working on the farm made me much stronger than they were. I would have preferred to be with an English group because I got along really well in training with the English-speaking guys. I was not used to the Quebecois because I grew up among English Canadians in Northern Alberta. These guys took every opportunity to berate me.

"It was difficult at times to work as a team because the other Alouettes all stuck together. Our wireless operator was in a different part of the plane, and the pilot was constantly talking. I wasn't used to sitting for so long, but it was an experience sitting in the turret and taking off into the air going forward but looking backward. Sitting backward on Old Blue when I was not much more than a toddler didn't quite prepare me for this.

"When we took off, I watched the runway as it gradually stretched out behind me, appearing to narrow the further we went and as the perspective changed. When taking off, the tail of the bomber lifts up first, so essentially I was the first one in the air although I was in the back of the plane. I had much more experience with horses, very little experience with cars, and no experience with planes. Joining the RCAF at times seemed like a holiday, and I was getting paid! That was a new experience for me because I wasn't paid for my work on the farm. My father never spoke to me, and I was too timid to complain. By joining the Air Force, I was able to make my own way and my own friends and to learn to perform in a way that would not have happened had I stayed on the farm."

"That must have been a tremendous learning experience for you."

"On many levels."

"Well, in spite of all the challenges I imagine you faced, you were able to put it all together because you are still here."

"Yes, I was able to acquire the skills I needed to perform my job. Learning to keep a careful watch of what was going on around me in the dark night skies and being able to spot aircraft and identify them when they were not much more than a dot in the sky was of the utmost importance. As soon as I spotted the enemy approaching us from behind, I became the captain, giving orders for evasive action. The pilot had to be ready to dive to port or starboard to avoid the attacking fighter plane.

The Alouette Squadron 425

"For these maneuvers, we trained during the day and it was just as intensive as anything we did at night. I was always looking around from my position in the turret. We only had Browning machine guns as weapons which were like peashooters, only effective to 500 yards, after which the bullets would become like rain. I was trained to listen and look, learning everything about the different activities around us and how to identify them. It was a new world for me and gave me a challenge I was more than ready to accept. However, such concentration for hours on end meant complete exhaustion for me and the rest of the crew upon our return to base. I knew the enemy fighters would try to approach to a distance from us of about one thousand yards in order to shoot. They knew I could only shoot up to 500 yards so they had a huge advantage over us. My job was to see them before they saw us. Therefore, it was less dangerous in some ways to conduct our missions at night as long as we could identify the enemy before they saw us. But it was also trickier identifying our bombing targets in the dark because of the blackouts. Nevertheless, given our equipment handicaps, it was the only way.

"The training was as intense as our missions would be. We had to be ready to dive or move to port or starboard to avoid the oncoming fighter plane, forcing one to hang on for dear life! Our training for evasive action took a lot of courage. Most of the crew was in the front of the plane; and of course, I was in the back getting tossed around with the mid-air gunner. He was never much help because I don't think his training 'took.' He fell through the cracks. One night, there was an enemy aircraft that he mistook for a Lancaster. The mid gunner said to the pilot, 'I think that a Lancaster is approaching.' When the pilot looked out the window in the direction of the approaching plane, he could clearly see the swastika on its side in the pitch dark. It was that close. The guy never opened fire. I don't know if he ever cocked his guns but he certainly didn't admit it. It would have been funny if he hadn't been risking our lives!

"As part of our training in Stafford-upon-Avon, we went on 'nickel raids' dropping all over France propaganda leaflets that looked like cigarette papers. In order to have them land where we wanted, we dropped altitude and let them go. They were designed to fly around and land in the largest area possible. It was just as dangerous as a bombing mission because of our position at the low altitude there were a lot of explosions around us from the bombs that were dropped by our Bomber Command. It was nerve-wracking flying back to base with punctures in the airplane from the flying debris of the explosions. These big pieces of shrapnel from shells that were approximately four inches squared were capable of causing dangerous gaps in the metal skin of the plane. If we returned to base with damage, the planes were hustled quickly into a big hangar to be out of sight and where the repairs could be quickly completed for the aircraft to be available for service the next day.

"More collateral damage was caused by the millions of bullets that fell out of the skies to the ground. The fields were covered with bullets that were ingested by the animals grazing in the pastures. Lead poisoning was not uncommon. War can have unintended consequences in unexpected places.

"We were at war and the minute we finished our training, we were expected to engage with the enemy fighters. The enemy fighters would fly in high above us trying to spot us from the advantage of their Spitfires. At that time, the enemy was much better equipped than we were, with faster planes and larger guns with ammunition that went farther and hit harder than ours. We had to make sure we spotted them before they found us so that we could both do our job and avoid their gunfire through evasion. It was necessary to begin scanning the skies the minute I took my position in the turret and we were airborne. The slightest inattention on my part could mean disaster for all of us."

Marcel's Turret Equipped with 303 Guns

Chapter 13

'May your life be as long as a river
unless it dries up!'
– Marcel Croteau

"When I came home from the war, it was expected that I would return to farming but I never did. My sons are so thankful that I did not. They had no interest in farming. It worried me that I might raise them the way I was raised but I was going to try my best to make sure that didn't happen. By then, farming was becoming highly mechanized and a lot of money was required to start up. It was also a very risky business in many ways besides financially."

"I think a lot of us today don't understand how resourceful farmers needed to be in the past in order to survive. And how much really hard, physical work was involved and how dependent you were on the weather for your crops. There were also a lot of physical dangers you encountered on a daily basis."

"A good example of weather effects was a big hailstorm that came and wiped out all our crops in the summer of 1935, right in the middle of the Depression. It happened on July 28th. It was on the same day as one of my sisters celebrated her birthday, so I remember that day very well.

"I also have a vivid recollection of another hailstorm. The cattle were out in the pasture almost a mile from home when a thunderstorm came rolling across the prairie. As the thunder and lightning started striking around them, the cows and the bull made a beeline for a grove of trees. They crowded together under the trees because they instinctively felt they would be protected from the pelting hailstones. Which was true but unfortunately they did not know that lightning is attracted to the highest point in the landscape, in this case, the trees, under which they were standing.

"My father was already there with the animals, trying to get them out from under the trees when I rode up on Old Blue. Needless to say, the cattle were quite agitated and did not want to move, especially the bull who was very protective of the cows. I knew that a bull could knock a horse to the ground and that eye injuries and goring of the body could happen to the rider if he tangled with the bull. My horse was trying desperately to get out of the rain and hail by joining the cattle under the trees thus thwarting my attempts to hold him back. I could hear the bull breathing heavily and snorting while my father used a three-pronged pitchfork to make him move. I was only seven or eight at the time and was terrified of the hail, the bull who didn't have a chain in his nose and the slough in the middle of the trees that was filling up with water. Whatever my father might have felt, he showed no fear and never panicked. Luckily, the storm left as quickly as it came, and we were thankful that there were no injuries to us or the animals."

*****

"In Alberta, long distances were traveled by train. By 1929, train service was extended to our community. It was quite a blessing for the farmers as it eliminated the need to travel 60 miles by horse and wagon to take their produce, hogs and cattle to market and their grain to the grain elevators where it was sold to the Alberta Wheat Board. That trek was always fraught with hazards. Navigating the steep hills with a heavy load was a challenge. Going downhill was the worst because in spite of the careful use of the brakes the wagon had a tendency to push the horses forward. Two teams of horses, one in front of the other, were required for the trip, and the driver had to be careful to let them travel at their own pace. In the winter, sleighs with wooden runners, which were even more difficult to handle than the wagons, were used with the horses. Fortunately, the drivers were quite skilled at the task.

"When my father made these trips, he was often gone for five to six days. He spent the nights sleeping in the wagon or sleigh. A buffalo coat kept him warm in winter."

*****

"When I was a little kid, about three or four years old, my brother and I walked together to visit Dad, who was out plowing in a field. This sibling was three years older than me, and I trailed behind him, as we walked about a kilometer along the main road to reach the field where our father was working. I remember watching Dad coming toward us with a plow and five horses. This was new land that my dad had cleared for cultivation. There was a pile of logs stacked between two fields. Under the logs there were two logs crossed over each other which created a small space under them. The logs were about 25 feet away from where my father was working. As we approached the woodpile, my brother thought he saw some movement. He grabbed a stick from some debris left from clearing trees from the land, to poke into the logs. Suddenly, to our surprise, we heard a hissing noise and a lynx jumped out at us. I was standing behind my brother but just as he turned around to run, the lynx leaped at me and bowled me over. The lynx immediately returned to its hiding place under the logs. She did not run away which indicated that probably she was a mother guarding her kittens, although we did not see them. When my dad saw what was happening, he quickly left the plow, grabbed a big stick, and ran toward the hiding lynx. It hissed at him too. There was nothing to be done so Dad said, 'Let's just go home.' Which is what we did. That was one of the most terrifying events of my life!"

"Were you scratched by the lynx?"

"I don't remember."

"Well, it is remarkable that you have this memory from such a young age."

"Having a wild animal jump out at me left an intense impression on me and made me very fearful for a long time. I was further traumatized when the neighbors would come for a visit and talk about their lynx and wolf experiences. The children listened and were frightened because when the adults would tell their stories, we never knew for sure if they were fact or fiction. I don't know if the adults realized how much they were scaring the little kids.

"My dad used to tell us stories not to scare us but to warn us and equip us with healthy fears that would protect us. A traumatic fear created at a young age stays with you. My story about walking alone across the fields and forests going home from school illustrates this well. Everywhere I looked, I could see lynx and wolves watching me, where in reality there were none.

"Overall my greatest fear was of lynx. One of my chores was to bring the wood we used for fuel into the house. If I didn't bring it in when there was daylight, my parents sent me out in the dark to the woodpile. Every black shadow I saw out there was a lynx. I had such a vivid imagination that sometimes I would pick up an armful of wood and I would think I saw a shadow and I would drop the wood and run into the house empty handed. That usually occurred on dark winter nights when everything was white with snow. I wasn't frightened in the summer because landscape was dark and I couldn't distinguish places where lynx might be hiding."

"It seems to me your encounter with the lynx taught you a new skill: to be very vigilant of your surroundings."

"Yes. To be able to concentrate and observe everything around me proved to be invaluable to me during my service in the war."

*****

"Earlier you spoke of having an uneven gait from a childhood injury that was visible during training to march when you were in boot camp. Was that from an injury on the farm?"

"It was actually an injury that happened to me at school. During lunch break at school one day, my friend who was also named Marcel and I were playing hide and seek. I think I was about eight years old. The teacher was out for lunch. We ran down the hall and up some stairs together to hide. We were both very athletic and ran fast. There was a closed in area at the top of the stairs in a corner where the roof hung over. We thought we could hide in there not realizing that broken glass was being stored there. The piece of glass closest to me was a long shard shaped like a spear. My friend waited outside the enclosed area while I ran in. I hadn't seen the glass and ran right into the exposed piece that was pointed at me. I was shocked when the speed of my run caused the glass shard to severely slash my leg to the bone. That day, I was wearing my suit that I usually wore to church. Mother bought my suit with two pairs of long pants and one pair of short pants. Both long pants were worn out so I had on my short pants. It was April so it seemed like a good idea. As it turned out, it was a very good thing I was wearing shorts or I would have been seriously reprimanded for ruining a pair of pants! I backed up from the glass that had penetrated my leg and felt it tearing my flesh. I held my leg around the injury and started walking down the stairs, blood pouring out and dripping on the treads. My teacher was summoned and as soon as she saw my wound and all the blood, she passed out on the floor. It didn't seem that she was going to be much help but fortunately she revived quite quickly and went to get some towels. She then used the towels to tightly wrap my leg and secured them with pins."

"It's lucky you didn't nick an artery."

"My leg was packed well with towels and a tourniquet was tied around my leg so it stopped bleeding. I think my teacher did a good job. Someone hitched the buggy that was at the school and drove me home. After the winter there were frost heaves and potholes everywhere in the road. The mail truck used to get stuck all the time in the dirt roads. The buggy bounced along the road as the driver tried to minimize the jostling over every bump or hole in the road that sent a jolt of pain up my leg. The kind driver had to walk back to the school because Dad needed the buggy to drive me to the hospital. Our model T Ford was on blocks. We couldn't use it in the spring because the roads were so bad. Smooth, usable roads were only a dream.

"The doctor who had a practice in Bonnyville was involved in a family feud involving his wife's brother and a girl that was such a scandal he had to move to St. Paul, twenty five miles away. The road between Bonnyville and St. Paul was not navigable so the doctor took the train to Bonnyville every two weeks to treat his patients. Meanwhile, I was in the hospital being attended to by the nuns who were not qualified nurses but did offer nursing care. By the time the doctor arrived ten days later, the cut had healed, so it was never sewn up, leaving me with a hole in my leg. That was more or less typical of the medical care that was available at the time in small prairie communities.

"There was so much work to accomplish on the farm that I could not have my injured leg prevent me from performing my chores for long. When I returned home after ten days in the hospital, I still couldn't walk on my leg. Fortunately, we had a little red wagon. To get around, I put my knee of my injured leg in the wagon and pushed with my other leg. My older brother was not about to let me abandon my duties so he came to me and said, 'You have to milk the cows too! You are pretending.' He was always supervising and watching me as if he were my guardian angel (but a dark one at that)! After a few days at home, the worst was over and I could carry out my duties more easily."

*****

"After school, I regularly unhitched from the buggy our 24-year-old horse named Old Blue who took us to and from school. He and I rode out to the pastures to bring home the cows that had spent the day there grazing. We had 150 cattle and 160 acres of pasture with a little lake on it where the cattle and our big bull that weighed almost a ton, drank. He was always sitting in the middle of the pasture watching me with the cows. Fortunately, my old horse was always looking after me. I could have gone anywhere with him but I was afraid of the bull. Some of the animals, including the bull, had rings in their noses. Occasionally a chain, which we used to guide the animal, was threaded through the ring causing the creature to walk slightly sideways. That was somewhat difficult for the animals, but we felt safer having more control over them when we had to go on foot and especially when the bull was among us. I usually stayed quite far behind sending Barney after the cattle and hollering my instructions to him from my position. When the cattle saw the dog, they started to move toward home because they knew from experience he would nip a few of them if they did not go. The cows occasionally ran ahead around some bushes and then stood on the other side of a fence in the green fields waiting for more instructions. I was glad when the bull stayed in the pasture and didn't come with us. Barney nipped at them again if they stopped, exercising his position as 'boss.' Arriving at our destination, I always felt a great sense of relief. When I started fetching the cows, I think I was about seven."

"Didn't your parents ever worry about your safety with those large animals?"

"No. There were ten more of us!"

Chapter 14

'The bravest are surely those who have
the clearest vision of what is before them,
glory and danger alike, and yet go out to meet it.'
– Pericles

"You have faced a lot of danger and fear in your life as a child and as an adult which you somehow seem to have overcome."

"Well, I don't think fear is something that you can overcome or make disappear. But it is an emotion that you can learn to manage. For example, each time we went on a mission, I felt afraid until we got into the air and I was able to concentrate on the job I had to do. My job was spotting the enemy and either giving commands for evasive action or firing my guns. I really didn't have time to be afraid.

"It was difficult as a child growing up on a very large farm where the work never seemed to end. I didn't have an easy life, quite unlike the simpler lives I suspected the kids in the city had. My childhood experiences, though, were integral in preparing me for my role in combat. When we were pursued or attacked by the enemy, as the rear gunner, I had to be able to quickly identify them, which was not easy because they looked like a fly in the night sky. However, I soon learned to keep up with their movements by blinking my eyes and constantly surveying the night sky. Luckily, none of them were ever able to open fire on us, as we avoided them by evasive action. We never wanted them to get near us because we knew where the firepower was and we knew our limits.

"Combat was not the only hazard we faced, although, it was arguably the most dangerous. Some nights we would lose 100 bomber aircraft but the average was about 5% per mission. There were a lot of other hazards when flying in Bomber Command. Many of the planes that were designed and built and then modified during the war were problematic. The bomb bay, the wings, and the body formed the basic structure. The most minor problem was that there were no cushions on the seats. We were sitting on hard surfaces which were metal not wood and very cold to sit on especially when we were flying at high altitudes. It never occurred to me at the time to bring a newspaper to sit on and provide some insulation."

"What other hazards were there that one would not necessarily anticipate?"

"It was all hazards! I joined up as an Air Gunner. During the First World War, the air gunners often ended up accidentally killing each other. It was said their lives in combat lasted seven minutes. I didn't know what to expect. I didn't know anything about rear turrets. We trained in Canada in a turret on a fighter plane. One of the planes we flew for training purposes at Mont Joli, Quebec, was a single engine fighter from the late 1920s or early '30s. The fighter had the main turret in the back of the plane. The pilot had his seat in the front and then on the floor behind him was a hole 18 inches square meant to be an escape hatch if we had to bail or we crashed. In the case of a crash, we would need to land upside down in order to get out of that opening. There should have been flaps on it, but they were long gone. Two rear gunners were on board. One would go into the turret which was in the back of the plane by placing his feet on each side of the hole and bracing himself so he wouldn't fall through the hole while going into the turret to do the exercise. The other gunner would be standing by. Then, we would change positions. When we got out of the turret, one had to be careful not to fall through the escape hole. It wasn't very comfortable and it wasn't very safe but we did not dwell on it. These turrets were designed between WWI and WWII, sometime in the '30s. The mechanics of the machine guns were worn out and had not been serviced. We had to bang on the machine gun to put it in position. After we shot with it, it was so hot it burned my hand when I touched it. After that first time, it didn't happen again.

"When I went overseas, the Halifax bombers had the best turrets with a stick for control, like the stick a fighter pilot had, to maneuver the gun. I could easily control it. It was really fast and I quickly figured out how the whole thing operated so I never had any problems with the guns. After the Battle of Britain, the invasion and the defending of France the consequences of the battles were that most of the planes were full of holes that had been hastily patched up."

"I guess you had great air conditioning!"

"The planes were already cold enough, we didn't need more air flow.

"One of the hazards of war that not many survivors like to talk about is the use of performance enhancing drugs. In fact, it was a deep dark secret. Amphetamines and methamphetamine were developed around 1934 and were 'recommended' for use by Bomber Command and other sections of the armed forces. At the time, amphetamines were sold as an inhaler called Benzedrine for use as a decongestant. The dark secret was that they were used extensively during the war as a stimulant and performance enhancer. After all, most missions for us occurred in the middle of the night so these drugs were deemed necessary. I was 'encouraged' to take them but had an allergic reaction which made me very agitated and aggressive so that was the end of that experiment for me.

"In England, we had a lot training in ground school. There were no mechanics to service the guns, so we had to learn how to do it. The blueprints for the guns were all on the wall in the classroom and the instructors were gunners that had finished their tours. Not everybody had the ability to be an instructor. Our instructor got stuck in the middle of one of our sessions. He couldn't move. He just froze. Then, he said, 'Can anybody help me?' So I offered because I knew every part and how it worked. When I looked at the blueprints, it just came to me although I had never seen blueprints like that before. I was able to explain how the guns worked."

"What did your instructor say when you finished?"

"Well, I don't remember but I received good marks! I didn't realize it at the time, but our instructor probably had Post Traumatic Stress Disorder. He had flown during WWI in the old bombers which were much more dangerous than those I flew in. There weren't many survivors in those days. They called those bombers, 'the flying coffins.' That's what they were. I think all the work I did on the farm made me practical. I sat on the sulky driving eight horses with the plow or the harrows or the mowers or the rake, I drove two teams, one in each hand to pick up a ton of hay every twenty minutes and made a new haystack. So I had learned some skills like coordination and problem solving, but I didn't realize that at the time."

"So you deciphered these blueprints without having worked with any kind of machinery or blueprints before?

Obviously you had a great deal of innate ability to be able to interpret these blueprints."

"True. I had a grade 9 education with C- marks! I had to do chores in the morning and after school so I never had time to do my homework. I was zonked out by the time we were free from our chores to do homework. Well, you know later on when I went into the construction business, I drew all the blueprints for my projects. I started with a protractor and a big ruler on a table and I taught myself how to do it.

"Our first missions were bombing industrial Germany. Then, we started bombing targets in France as we were softening up German defenses for the Normandy invasion. We carried out tactical bombing of bridges and military installations.

"My very first mission was carried out on the night before Christmas Eve, 1943. Our orders sent us to Manheim, Germany. We were flying over France on our way to the target when I spotted an enemy fighter approaching us. I gave instructions for evasive action which were followed by a huge bang. It seems the pilot by mistake had gone into an evasive dive that was too steep and too fast which caused the plane to loop. That means we were flying upside down until the pilot could come out of the loop and upright the plane. The force of the loop caused me to hit the ceiling, and I split my head open. We were wearing aviator caps. I was in the turret where all the rivets were on the inside of the panels and there was an edge along a seam. That's what I hit. I never reported that injury, I just wiped off the blood that was on the cap. I remember later when I took it off some of my hair was coated in blood.

Stratford-Upon-Avon Operational Training Unit
First Mission December 22/23 1943

"Our pilot never admitted that he had looped the plane, it was a very dangerous maneuver and too embarrassing to talk about. At night, when there are no lights and it is all darkness, you can lose your bearings and with no reference points, you are not able to tell which way is up. There is a danger of stalling the plane which would be a real hazard when it is loaded with bombs. I talked to some other pilots after the war who admitted they had looped too, so it was a common problem. Minutes after the pilot corrected the loop, we were attacked by a Messerschmidt BF-109, a German fighter aircraft that was the backbone of the Luftwaffe's fighter force. It was a single engine plane considered to be the finest and deadliest of all WWII fighter planes. Somehow, we managed to evade and avoid an encounter with this superstar.

"The adrenaline was still pumping when we returned to base. I consumed much more than my share of libations that night and can remember being so hot I went outside and laid in the frost covered grass to cool off. Not surprising, my drinking buddies and I were not able to make it to Christmas dinner the next day.

"Our crew was a diverse group. Our excellent pilot was from Magog, Quebec, the navigator was a schoolteacher from Montreal, the engineer from Fort William, and the bombardier was from a small town in Ontario. The upper gunner had been brought up in an orphanage and was difficult to deal with. These guys didn't have the work or responsibilities that I had on the farm, so it was like a different culture for me. I could have been with a Russian crew, and it would have been easier for me because the Russians were mostly farmers.

"In England, we were crewed up and between schooling and sleeping we would be flying for bombing practice. Every time we took off, the gunner had to be to be in the airplane. The bullets the Germans used were 55 mm in size and mine were pencil size, about 9 mm. We had peashooters, and the Germans had canons. Because of this, we had to learn to take evasive action to make up for our lack of firepower. Nevertheless, I won seven air battles. Obviously, we won all the battles we were engaged in or we would not have survived. When the enemy was close enough for me to fire, I didn't miss."

"I don't know quite how to ask this question, but there is something puzzling me about all these kids going to war. You were 19 or 20. Why is it always kids that go to war and are they the only ones who are willing to put themselves in such danger?"

"I was 19 when I enlisted in April 1942. I was in training from August 1942 onward to December 1943. We were all just kids. It's like sports, you get to a certain age, and then you're too old for the game. When you are young, your reflexes are better, your eyesight is better. Shooting down an enemy airplane was like scoring a home run to win the American baseball pennant."

"So how many missions did you engage in?"

"I completed 39 missions.

Arriving at the Airport

"When we were finally ready for combat, there was a routine we generally followed for each mission. We ate our pre-mission meal, nicknamed 'the last supper,' went to our briefing, and then we dressed in our flying clothes. Then, we gathered up our parachutes and harnesses and climbed into a lorry which was something like a jeep but a bit longer. It could seat twenty men in the back and was equipped with a trailer behind it that carried the bombs. Next, we were driven out to the planes that were sitting on the tarmac. When we returned from our missions, they would pick us up with the lorry and ambulances. There were 11 people working on the ground for every person in the air. Each squadron would be taken to the airfield. It was usually late in the day, as we were preparing for night missions. The planes were all lined up on the tarmac waiting for the signal that the weather was clear enough to leave. There were reconnaissance planes flying over Germany that wired back the weather reports. If there were heavy clouds, we might have to wait two or three hours, sometimes longer, for the signal to go. As soon as we received the signal, we climbed into the planes and started the motors. The space on the tarmac allowed for parking all the planes. There were 24 planes in each squadron and two squadrons on each base, one squadron lined up on each side of the tarmac. They alternated sides for takeoff. As the first plane took off, the next one would line up and wait for the green light to take off. When the runway was cleared, 48 planes were heading to our night bombing destination.

Waiting for Take-off

"Once airborne, if there were two cloud formations and 1,000 feet clear between them, the pilot would try to would climb through that hole. However, we never seemed to find those spaces. The weather changed so quickly. When we finally took off and got to 10,000 feet, we headed to France or Germany, eventually climbing to 18,000 or 20,000 feet. We flew into the darkness, literally and figuratively, because the sun was setting in the west and we were flying eastward. Flying at night was very dangerous. We didn't have any visual landmarks, and the pilot could easily become disoriented. Fortunately, our pilot knew what he was doing. So did the navigator who charted our path using the stars. There was no radar. It was much safer flying on a moonlit night but it left us exposed to the enemy. Our wireless operator listened to the radio and took all the messages and the weather reports, including temperatures and wind direction and velocity. That was basically it for the technology available to us.

By the time we got to our destination, it was pitch black. I had to be alert, watching constantly. Sitting in the turret, I was at the back of the plane facing backward keeping watch for any enemy planes trying to sneak up behind us. There was no point in the enemy approaching us from the front because at the speeds both planes were flying, we would just fly past each other with no time to engage in combat.

"When an enemy was spotted, I became the captain, and the pilot had to follow my instructions. My running commentary with the pilot gave him directions to dip his wings to the port or starboard if there was a plane coming in underneath or any other instructions needed to evade or confront the enemy. That was the part of my job which the crew in the front found reassuring because they knew I was there doing my job. My pilot was amenable to our arrangement but some pilots were not. I flew once with a Commissioned Officer who said to me, 'Gunner, don't move your guns,' because he had the plane on autopilot. I just sat there, it was like being in a jail cell. There was nothing I could do but watch. He wasn't cooperating with us. He was a crew captain and was fond of giving orders. That night when we were flying over the channel, we met two German fighters. Of course, we were in a stream of bombers, and the bombardier told us they were coming in behind us. I was getting ready to shoot, but the crew captain said, 'Don't shoot.' I remember the words ringing in my ears. I was ready to shoot the minute the enemy appeared. That's what I was there for. We were going one way and the enemy was flying perpendicular to us, so I was prepared to shoot so that he would fly into my mist of bullets."

"That must have been very difficult. How did you learn to do that?"

"On the farm, I used to shoot partridges, prairie chickens, and wild ducks. I never had a shotgun so I used a 22 rifle and I had to shoot at them in flight. In the fall, my Sunday afternoons were spent in the fields hunting the waterfowl with my dog. When I enlisted, I already had lots of practice shooting guns. When you shoot at a flying duck, you have to shoot ahead of the bird so that it flies into the bullet or into the pellets. If you waited too long to shoot, the target would fly by and the ammunition would cross the target's path too late. After the war, I went hunting with my shotgun and I frequently encountered other people hunting in the fields. I had a shotgun that would shoot twice as far as the other hunters' guns. I positioned myself behind them and shot over their heads, hit the bird, and yelled, 'It's a gift!' as it fell out of the sky. I was hiding in the bushes by the fences, so they never saw me.

"When we bombed industrial Germany, we went with 1,000 planes and a seven or eight man crew in each plane. One night, we lost 104 planes in one night. At the time, weather forecasting wasn't very reliable. On this occasion, there was a 100 mph tail wind from the south that sent the planes off course and into the North Sea. As they ran out of gas, they perished. It was the worst fate landing on the ocean because you can't ditch safely when the waves are that high. The aircraft catapults when it hits the water, so there were a lot of casualties. There were 54,000 total casualties in Bomber Command and almost 15,000 men were Canadians who lost their lives. That's the highest losses in both great wars, more than the army and navy if you count only the aircrews.

"The bombing of Dresden is well documented and well known. It's not generally known that the bombing of Hamburg was much worse. We were sent there on a bombing mission one night. It was a moonlit sky, adding to the danger of our trip because it would be difficult to evade the enemy if we were spotted. When we arrived at our target, there were explosions everywhere. The Germans had searchlights, cones of light flashing in the night sky and reaching 40,000 feet in the air. These cones of light were used to illuminate the enemy planes so that the Germans could shoot them down. We got coned in Hamburg and the only way to get out of it was to dive into it, which we did. The lights went out, their radar lost track of us and we escaped!"

"Did you ever wonder why you chose to be air crew when it was well known to be the most dangerous job?"

"No. I never questioned it, because that's what I wanted to do. I wanted to fly. I didn't spend a lot of time thinking about my mortality, I just did my job. There were quite a few survivors when I finished our last mission on September 13, 1944. I remember that date because it was a Friday the 13th!"

"Okay, let's go back to your missions."

"One night, we were waiting on the tarmac to begin our mission. As soon as the green light signaled, one after the other, each plane prepared for take-off. I was in my position in rear turret when our turn came to leave. We were going forward, but I was facing backward and because of the speed that we were traveling to get airborne, I was being pulled to the back. That's the sensation I had as the pilot lifted the tail and I was the first one airborne. When he got enough speed, he pulled the tail down and lifted the front. Meanwhile, I was looking at the runway as it zipped by, and while we were taking off, a flame flashed by my turret. The starboard engine was on fire. I yelled, 'Fire in starboard engine!!!' The pilot immediately cut the burning engine, but we were at the point of no return for taking off. He couldn't take off as fast as he needed and went right to the end of the runway before becoming airborne. He was trying to hold the aircraft steady but because one motor out of four was incapacitated, it was too difficult to maneuver the plane to return to the runway. There were trees below us that we just missed brushing as we became airborne. I felt like I could reach out and touch them, as we took off over the city of York. I saw people in the street watching us going overhead, barely missing treetops. I could almost see the white of their eyes! We had to just keep going, skimming over rooftops. The pilot couldn't maneuver the plane because it was too low and the air was still. It's much easier to take off and fly if there is wind. He didn't have any chance to fly higher, and we were too low to bail out so we continued on toward the Yorkshire Mountains, not very confident that we could ever land safely.

"Our pilot managed to turn slightly toward a valley where he could gain some height and then turn to head out over the mountains and fly to the sea. We flew about two hours at 2400 feet to the ocean where we dropped our bombs, half of which exploded on impact. The ocean was full of bombs as a result of similar events. It was either that or you died. You can't land safely with bombs and three motors. We also flew for a while to reduce the amount of fuel in preparation for landing. The sweat was running down my body, as we prepared to land. I had seen too many accidents with planes burning at the end of the runway because the same thing had happened to many others. We came home in radio silence but because the airport was lit up, we landed safely. Fortunately, our pilot had nerves of steel.

"There were quite a few other close calls. On another occasion, we were taking off with a load of bombs. One motor was overheating because we were overloaded with big supplementary tanks filled with gas on both sides of the airplane. The pilot was losing one motor and couldn't climb. To get over the channel to the coast of France you had to be at a certain altitude which our pilot could not achieve. For that reason, the pilot decided to turn around and head back to our base. We had used up some gas but we dumped more along with our bombs into the English Channel. If we crashed with those overloaded tanks, we would not survive. With some trepidation, we returned to the base and landed safely in front of the CO whom I mentioned earlier.

"This was yet another PTSD inducing event. During WWI, after trials, they shot 12 Canadian soldiers whose only offence was having PTSD, not yet recognized. The English were pretty diligent on that front. At that time, it was called shell shock or lack of moral fiber (LMF) and one might be shot as a traitor. It was barbaric, but it was a common way of thinking at the time.

"One night, some of our crew went on a mission with the CO. We took off in a thunderstorm and flew through a bank of clouds where there was a lot of movement of air. It was like hitting a pile of rocks. Bang, bang. As before, the CO said to us, 'Gunners, hold your guns and remain in your turrets.' Following orders, I just sat there watching the storm happening around us. I had never seen anything like it. There was electricity in the air, little lightning strikes happening between my machine guns. Then, with a whoosh, it was gone. We flew over a German target that was a bombing site on the coast of France. It was a long trip. After bombing our target, we headed for home where we landed safely. The next morning, the ground crew came and reported to us that, much to our surprise, we had returned from our mission with all of our bombs. The previous night, the bombardier, who was from another crew, had said, 'Bombs gone,' but he forgot to put his master switch on so the bombs didn't drop. We had come home and landed with a whole load of bombs! The CO called the bombardier into his office and because he was a big guy, he grabbed the bombardier by the collar of his shirt and kicked him out the door but only after demoting him. Around the same time, this a guy got caught with a military motor in the trunk of his car so he went to jail. None of this reflected well on the CO, and I had to laugh because this CO acted like a bully around me, so for me, there was humor in the situation.

Besides, by then I was gaining confidence, following my decoration by the King."

Loading Bombs Tholthorpe,Yorkshire,England 1944

Taking off at Dusk for night bombing, flying East into the darkness at 21;45 0100 Shot down Enemy Aircraft JU88 in 3.5 seconds

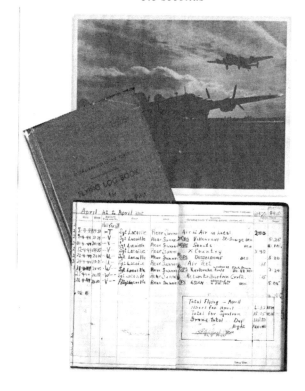

Chapter 15

'Only the dead will know the end of war.'

– Plato

"I grew up near the town of Bonnyville, a fairly remote community in northern Alberta, situated north of Edmonton and south of Cold Lake, near the Saskatchewan border. During the time period that I lived on the farm, there were many challenges and obstacles that had to be overcome just to survive from day to day. We had to be individually and collectively resourceful. We also had to be able to get along with our neighbors because we depended on each other for help during times of trouble, emergencies of any type and also for our social activities. Because there were many branches of each family living in proximity to one another, we were a closely-knit group. Neighbors were often relatives. That, however, did not prevent the petty jealousies, insecurities, occasional scandals, competitive attitudes, narrow-mindedness, and conflict experienced in most communities.

"One major disadvantage of our location was our lack of easily accessible adequate medical care. It was a long time into the future before Tommy Douglas and before a universal health care system for Canada would be created. Many medicines, like antibiotics, were not yet available. Our hospital, which was more like a nursing station or clinic, was staffed by nuns who did not have nursing qualifications but who did their best to care for the sick and injured. We did not always have a doctor available. One of my cousins was a victim of the lack of prompt medical care. One day, he became very ill and was incapacitated with a fever and a very sore neck. My aunt and uncle took him as soon as they could to the local hospital. The doctor was summoned from where he lived in St. Paul's, the nearest town, and took the train to Bonnyville to treat my cousin Paul. By the time the doctor arrived, my cousin had passed away. Paul, who was only nine years old, had succumbed to meningitis.

"All of our family, friends, and neighbors came to the funeral. The church was full for the service, and there were quite a few people standing outside. When I entered the church, my father, who was standing beside the coffin, motioned to me to come and stand beside him. I have this strange feeling right now just thinking about the experience. It was the first time I saw a dead body and I felt quite unnerved. I knew I had to get out of there as quickly as I could, hopefully as inconspicuously as possible while I hurried out of the church. Setting off for home, I fought the urge to run fearing I would attract attention. Therefore, I walked away as quickly as I could. I think it must have been June because there were many rosebushes blooming along the roadside. Because of my encounter with the lynx, I was very afraid of wild animals. My imagination was operating at full throttle and my fear overcame me. I picked up speed and ran almost a mile home just as fast as I could to escape the danger that lay all around me. I finally reached the house, ran upstairs, and threw myself into the safety of my bed. I could not catch my breath. That very scary event became one of my many secrets. I don't think I've ever told a soul. I was supposed to be brave. Therefore, I could not reveal to anyone that I might have a weakness. That was a lesson well learned. I have spent a great deal of time in my life hiding my thoughts and feelings in order not to reveal the genuine me."

"Your story of the loss of your cousin was tragic and had a profound effect on you. What was it like during the war and afterwards to lose friends on a regular basis?"

"It was very difficult. I knew that the British had been suffering huge losses when they first started to bomb Germany. Although it might have seemed like suicide, it did not deter me from enlisting. My first experience of personal loss at war was while we were still training in Pershore. My teacher's husband M. Gibeau was killed in a crash along with his whole crew. I knew all these guys who were suddenly gone. It was happening every day and we were still just in training! We had to learn quickly how to deal with these deaths. I tried to shut it out through distraction. Somehow, we were able to compartmentalize our actions and our thoughts although it was very difficult to do when we were surrounded by so much death and destruction. The repercussions would come much later. Many of the crashes happened at the end of the runway. The debris from those crashes was very quickly hauled away into a hanger so that as few as possible would see the remains. When we could, we held funerals for those that we lost and together we carried the caskets on our shoulders."

"I am so sorry to be upsetting you with my questions. I can see how much this has affected you."

"I have buried this for a very long time and now it's all coming out. It's very painful to talk about, but I have swept a lot of tragedies under the carpet, and it's time they come out into the light of day.

"We got to know many of the other crew members, most of whom came from the cities and many who didn't really belong in the service. There was one fellow whose name was Gold. He was a classical musician so whenever he was available he entertained us by playing the piano in the mess hall. He also sang songs which were a wonderful distraction for us. There were all kinds of moments that were thrilling for us. We also watched movies every night. These activities were supposed to help us get our heads back together after an operation. There was usually a great big barrel of beer on a table in the mess hall and we were encouraged to drink as much as we wanted. We learned how to use alcohol to cope with the horrors of war.

"Each airman was given a tweed jacket, a pair of trousers, a shirt, and a tie. They were meant to be taken with us on each operation so that if we were shot down and survived, we would have clothes to wear if we had to hide somewhere in France. None of my crew ever wore them and neither did I. It seemed too much like we were asking for trouble. However, this guy Gold wore his civilian clothes all the time. He was a bombardier and Jewish and was terrified of being captured by the Germans."

"It seems you have to be careful what you ask for because you might get it and find it might not turn out to be what you want."

"I've done that one too many times in my life. At the time, I didn't know what was happening to the Jews in Europe so I didn't fully understand the depth of his fear. One night, Gold and his crew flew in just after we had landed. We were right there on the tarmac when they crash-landed. A bomb went off. The rear turret fell like a stone from the plane and flew across the tarmac and crashed into the hangar. Some of the airmen got blown out of the aircraft, but the rear gunner was trapped in the turret. The air commodore ran to his car to find an axe with which to free the gunner. As he ran to the turret, another bomb went off, and his arm was torn off by some shrapnel. He was the CO of the Canadians. Another air gunner was able to free the trapped gunner. The rescued gunner grabbed his savior so gratefully and hung on so tightly that he almost strangled him. It had been our habit to always smoke a cigarette the minute we got out of the plane after a mission. Therefore, it was not unusual as soon as he was freed from the turret to ask for a cigarette. I lit one for him and handed it to him. He took one drag and died. That was gut wrenching. I knew one of the two guys who survived that crash. He had red hair. I met him by accident because he was in a different squadron, the OWLS and we didn't usually co-mingle. When I went on leave, I met him a few times. He was one of the lucky ones who made it through the war because I ran into him once in London. I wondered at the time what demons he carried from his experiences.

"Another enlisted man I was friends with was Gagnon, a guy I met at St. John's where I was enrolled in grade nine. We were in training together as gunners and became good friends. It was not uncommon for counterparts from different crews to room together. Gagnon and I were paired as roommates. One night, I came back to base at 2 a.m. with my crew after a long training mission. A plane crashed and burned in a field close to the airport, as we were going to our debriefing. We took off our parachutes and our flying clothes in the cloakroom before going into the adjacent room. All of us were quite sure we knew which crew had crashed and assumed they had all been killed. After our debriefing, we went to the mess hall for a meal where we learned that six of the eight-man crew had been killed, two survived the crash. A short while later when I went back to my room, some MP's were walking out with Gagnon's kit bag and the remainder of his possessions. It wasn't difficult to figure out what had happened. It was a severe blow to acknowledge that he was dead. Two weeks later, I received a letter from a nurse who worked in a special military hospital. She wrote it on behalf of Gagnon who was asking me to send his stuff to him. Apparently, he was the sole survivor of the crash and had a head injury that was repaired with stainless steel plates. I wrote back to him to tell him that, after the crash, the MPs had walked out of our room with his belongings just as I was returning."

"It must have been a shock to find out he was still alive."

"It was. His pilot had trained with my pilot, so we were a pretty close-knit group. I never heard from Gagnon again until much later when I ran into him in Edmonton on the steps of the legislative building where he worked. He said hello, we briefly chatted, and he moved on. Later on, my brother-in-law who lived in the same town as Gagnon told me he never said more than a few words to anyone. It sounded like he was living in his own kind of hell. Poor man!"

"It's terrible that as survivors of the war you came home after having seen all these horrible things and there was no help for you nor the understanding from others that you had suffered such trauma."

"We knew something was wrong with us but we didn't understand what it was. No one did. I blamed myself for my behavior. When we went home, those around us thought we were crazy and tried to make sense of us but could not, so they called us jerks. I had a good relationship with some of these guys but others, not so much. Fights were often the end result.

"Other friends who disappeared were upper gunners with whom I had trained and who went into action before me. Because I was a rear gunner, I required more training than they did. By the time I joined my squadron, these guys had already been shot down. We usually lost about 5% of the squadron every night, so after 20 missions, none of us should still have been alive.

"I found out much later that one friend who disappeared was a prisoner of war. He survived and eventually went home and studied to be a lawyer or a doctor, I'm not sure which. When I was back home in early July of 1945, he came to visit me while I was in the hospital recovering from surgery for appendicitis. (I later found out my appendix was normal. I still periodically have the same pain in my side when I talk about the war, a symptom of my post-traumatic stress disorder, PTSD.) That was the last time I saw him. He had a cabin on Moose Lake which was near Bonnyville. There was a commercial fishery on the lake and he apparently got tangled in some nets while swimming and drowned.

"My disturbing experiences were not just about the loss of my friends and acquaintances. They were also about the job I was required to do to fight the enemy. My job was to find a fly in the dark sky that was an enemy fighter which we did not want tracking us down. I needed to see them before they saw us. Fortunately, I had excellent night vision. I could find a mouse in the dark. As soon as I spotted the enemy, I would either give evasive action instructions to our pilot or I would shoot. If the enemy plane was in the right position at the right distance, I would fire my machine guns, 250 rounds in three and a half seconds or 70 rounds per second. I never missed and would shout to my crew, 'I just shot them! I got them! I got them!'

"The crew and I flew 39 missions and engaged in seven encounters with the enemy with deadly effect which in layman's terms means I shot them down. One night, I shot down a plane with three young kids in it about my age. By that time in the war, the Germans were short of pilots so they were using younger kids. I am sure they were thinking that they were doing the right thing defending their country from the bombing. Just as we thought we were doing the right thing for the right reasons."

"I think one of the worst things about war is that we send our young kids out there to do the fighting."

"War can be a big business, making a lot of money for some people. At the time, I could not allow myself to think about what I was doing. I had a job to accomplish and I did it. But I think about it now. A lot. Time and distance give you a much different perspective."

Chapter 16

'Bravery does not mean that you are not afraid.
It means you go ahead anyway and do your job.'
– Marcel Croteau

"You have shown me the medals that you were awarded for your service overseas. What was it like to have your actions in battle honored?"

"One day, I was walking into the gunnery office when I was approached by the adjutant, a military officer who aids superior officers. He stopped me and told me that the commander wanted to see me. I was very apprehensive, wondering what was going on and what the commander wanted. The adjutant accompanied me to the commanding officer's office while I worried about the need for an escort. Did he think I was going to run away?

"A few minutes later, we walked into the commander's office and I stood before him. He said, 'Croteau, congratulations, you've been awarded the Distinguished Flying Medal.' This farm boy from Alberta was speechless! A thrill ran down my spine. I was the first one in my squadron of 1500 men to get a citation. I was also the first gunner to get the award because I shot down an enemy fighter. The enemy fighters at night stayed out of our range. My guns were only 303s and the enemy had much larger caliber guns that could shoot much further than ours. We usually had to give evasive action to avoid their guns when we were out of our shooting range. Otherwise, I would use my guns, which is what I did when I saw this plane. I gave it a burst from my guns for 3 1/2 seconds which was enough to eliminate the fighter plane. Therefore, it was a citation for 'using my guns with deadly effect.' I was overwhelmed with emotion. After all, I was just the farm boy with a 22 rifle!"

"Little did you know when you were a kid that you were training for something more. How old were you when this you received the Distinguished Flying Medal?"

"I was 20. After our year of training, we received a diploma for our efforts. I never expected to earn medals. Right away, the commander gave me a ribbon representing my medal."

"Did you wear the ribbon on your uniform?"

"No. Ribbons were worn on battle dress.

"The surprises for me did not end there. Later on, in August, I was on leave and I received a telegraph. It contained orders to return by the next day to my squadron because I was going to be presented with the medal I had earned by his Majesty King George VI. I gathered my things and immediately left for York where our squadron's base was located. On my return, I stopped at a bar where the guys in my squadron went to drink. There was another gunner there who was a joker and a comedian. He kept buying me drinks so we really had a lot to drink and I got quite drunk. A bicycle was my form of transportation to navigate the several miles from the bar to the barracks. Obviously, in my condition, that mode of transportation wasn't going to work. My friend came to my rescue and took me to his accommodations where I spent the rest of the night being quite sick."

"This was the night before meeting the King. Were you hung over in the morning?"

"When I got up the next morning, I felt very unwell. After my adventures the night before, my shoes were a mess. Luckily, I had two pairs of shoes but in order to wear the standby shoes, I had to find them first and then give them a good polishing."

"I have a very vivid picture in my mind that you are painting having raised three boys. Were you a little frantic getting ready?"

"It was as if I were in a different reality, getting ready to meet the King. In addition to polishing my shoes to a mirror shine, I needed to press my uniform to a crisp finish. I attempted to dress impeccably to honor my squadron and so no one would guess what turmoil was going on inside me. I had an empty stomach because I could only drink cold water. Food was definitely out of the question. I do not think I had ever in my life felt more horrible. Eventually, I finished getting ready and went out to the road to catch the bus to get to the ceremony. I spent the trip hunkered down trying to keep my head from exploding. There would be no escort for me to the presentation. No one else in the squadron was receiving a decoration that day, so I was on my own."

"With a pounding headache and an upset stomach, I am surprised you were able to get to the ceremony. What was it like meeting the King?"

"First I met with the guys from different squadrons who were getting medals. We were a little group who found ourselves being required to stand at attention for about two hours. I was parched and could have used another drink of water. The things that go through your head when you have a huge hangover!

"I felt sorry that King George had to do all that ceremonial stuff. No wonder he died young. I think the war was really hard on him. He was constantly making public appearances, like medal presentations and other events. It was clear that it must have been very difficult for him to be involved in a war where friends and members of the family (including his brother who abdicated the throne) were Nazi sympathizers and advisors. We never heard any comments about these people during the war. All the recipients stood tall and proud as their names were called. Suddenly, standing there feeling like I was ready to collapse, they called my name. I didn't know if I could stay on my feet but I bent my head forward and felt a little better. There was a little mat that we were to stand on for the presentation. I was not sure I could make my feet take me there without my falling down.

"To my great relief, I managed to present myself in front of the King. We were tutored regarding our conversation with the King. He was to ask the question: 'do you like the service?' The first words we were to say were 'Yes, Your Majesty' and the second we were to say was 'Sir!' I was so nervous I said 'Sir. Yes, Your Majesty.' I can still hear it in my head. My level of anxiety was exacerbated by my fatigue and lack of food. That was definitely one of those do-over moments.

"The picture of me with the King was sent home and it was hung on the flagpole in Bonnyville. I became a big hero. Friends and acquaintances would stop my parents on the street in their small town and ask my parents: 'Is that true?'

"My mother would say, 'Yes.' It seems to me that it was just a piece of luck that I happened to be there at the right time to do what needed to be done."

"*I think that a whole lot of training and ability kicked into action when you needed it.*"

"My experience of driving eight horses and a plow or other implement, keeping everything moving along and working came in handy. I could manage my guns with no problems. I also was not afraid of the enemy.

"Most of the squadron was from Quebec, they questioned what I was doing there with them. After all, I was just one of those cowboys from Western Canada. There were also many ways they found to make snide remarks concerning me and to turn up their nose at me. I was not one of them. They considered me to be from a different culture which was the worst of their attacks. We had a handicapped father who could not speak a word of English. He had a mental block. However, our family was as much French Canadian as any of them. I have a photo of my crew which shows me standing off to the side and the rest standing in front of our aircraft. A typical example of my relationship with most of the crew.

Royal Family & Brass, August 11th, 1944

Invested with award by King George August 11ᵗʰ, 1944

My Crew with Our Halifax Mark 3

"There were two squadrons on our base. The French Canadians were the Alouettes located on the north side of the airport. The south side of the airport was the location of the White Owls. When we were in the mess hall, we would sing the song *Alouette* and then we would sing *White Owl* to the same tune. Most of our antics were meant to help us forget what we did the night before and to not think about what was coming that night or the next. We were often given a day off because they didn't like us to fly two nights in a row. We had to sleep during the day when there always seemed to be too much noise around the barracks. Also, it was very difficult to sleep after we came back from a mission given our blood levels of adrenaline and amphetamines. Upon our return to base, it was our practice to take off our flying clothes and then head off to the debriefing. When we were finished there, we walked to the mess hall, which was about two miles away, followed by another mile-long trek back to our barracks."

"I guess that was a good exercise for you."

"Yes, we attempted to shake off the demons. The Alouettes maintained very high scores. We had the least losses, the most serviceable aircraft, and the most direct hits. I was the first air gunner in my squadron to shoot down a German plane and I was the first one to be decorated. There were quite a few who were decorated after me but not because they had shot down any planes but rather because they were French Canadians. It was decided by committee that each squadron would receive a certain number of decorations. The recipients appeared to have been picked at random. I knew of gunners who acquired a decoration without having fired a single shot with their guns. I was surprised to find politics involved in the honoring of life and death situations during the war. It seemed to me this practice belittled the whole idea of awarding medals."

"*What was the action that earned you the Distinguished Medal of Honor?*"

"Well, it was after my fifth mission that I shot down the enemy. Our crew really learned quickly and worked together well which allowed me to not fear the enemy. I did the job that was expected of me. We were about 15 or 20 minutes from our bombing target. I was looking all around me, surveying the night skies, and then suddenly the enemy was there and I reacted. Within seconds, the job was done."

"*Could you ever be prepared enough for something like that to happen?*"

"I think our intensive training prepared us to react quickly and effectively almost without thinking. My greatest fear was not being shot down by the enemy or dying but being interrogated by the Gestapo after being taken prisoner. That fear kept me alert."

"*You were good at your job.*"

"Every one of my crew was well trained."

"Recently, you were awarded the French Legion Medal of Honor, the highest medal awarded by the French Government. How did that come about?"

"A letter was sent to me from the Department of Veterans Affairs a few years ago informing me that I was qualified to apply for an honor from the French Government. There was a protocol I had to follow which involved taking my logbook to the President of the local Legion to have it verified. I had three operations just before D-Day, an operation on D-Day and after D-Day followed by operations on targets in Germany. Photos of all my WWII medals plus photos of me with King George IV were sent with my application. I received a phone call very shortly thereafter that I was going to be given the medal and rank of 'Knight of the Legion of Honor' right away. A perk of this honor from the French Government is an education at the Sorbonne in Paris for any of my progeny. I have 21 great-grandchildren.

"Not long afterwards, the beautiful, pure silver medal arrived in the mail. The medal was formally presented to me at a ceremony on April 28, 2014, attended by family and friends that was held at the Sechelt B.C. Canadian Legion. Looking at it and feeling the weight of my sterling silver medal in my hand, I thought perhaps I could melt it down!"

All Medals Awarded to Marcel, 1939-2014

Left to Right:

Distinguished Flying Medal 1935–45

Star Aircrew Europe Star Bar Representing Defense of France and Germany

Medal Defense of Britain

Medal Canadian Volunteer Service

Medal 1st Bar represents Bomber Command

Medal 2nd Bar represents Oversea Service

Medal of Victory

Medal Operational Wing for Gallant Service and Completion of Combat Tours

Knight of the Legion of Honor Medal from France.

George the Sixth, *by the Grace of God*

of Great Britain Ireland and the British Dominions beyond the Sea King Defender of the Faith, Emperor of India, &c

To Our Trusty and well beloved *Joseph Muriel Gilbert Cruveau* Greeting

We reposing especial Trust and Confidence in your Loyalty Courage and good Conduct, do by these Presents Constitute and Appoint you to be an Officer in Our Royal Canadian Air Force of Our Dominion of Canada from the *Second* day of *June* 19

You are therefore carefully and diligently to discharge your Duty as such in the Rank of *Pilot Officer* or in such other Rank as We may from time to time hereafter be pleased to promote or appoint you to of which a notification will be made in the Canada Gazette, or in such other manner as may for the time being be prescribed by Us in Council and you are in such manner and on such occasions as may be prescribed by Us to exercise and well discipline both the inferior Officers and other ranks serving under you and use your best endeavours to keep them in good Order and Discipline And We do hereby Command them to Obey you as their superior Officer and you to observe and follow such Orders and Directions as from time to time you shall receive from Us, or any your superior Officer in pursuance of the Trust hereby reposed in you.

In Witness Whereof Our Governor General of Our Dominion of Canada hath hereunto set his hand and Seal at Our Government House in the City of Ottawa this *First* day of *December* in the Year of Our Lord One Thousand Nine Hundred and *Forty four* and in the *Eighth* Year of Our Reign.

Pilot Officer Joseph Muriel Gilbert Cruveau, R.C.A.F.   By Command of His Excellency The Governor General

Royal Canadian Air Force

-Reserve - Special Section   for lheuten for

                                                            Minister of National Defence for Air

Letter to Marcel's Parents from Canada's Minister of National Defense for Air

CANADA

MINISTER OF NATIONAL DEFENCE FOR AIR

Mr. & Mrs. O.P. Croteau,   OTTAWA
Bonnyville,   June 22nd, 1944.
Alberta.

Dear Mr. & Mrs. Croteau:

        I am writing to say how much all ranks of the Royal Canadian Air Force join with me in warmly congratulating you and the members of your family on the honour and distinction which have come to your son Sergeant Joseph Marcel Albert Croteau DFM, through the award of the Distinguished Flying Medal for great gallantry in the performance of his duty while serving with No. 425 Squadron of the Royal Canadian Air Force.

        The citation on which this award was made reads as follows:

> "As rear gunner, this airman has participated
> in several sorties including attacks on such
> targets as Essen, Frankfurt and Karlsruhe.
> During the attack on the last named target,
> his aircraft was engaged by a fighter. Ser-
> geant Croteau used his guns with deadly effect,
> however, and his bullets set the enemy aircraft
> on fire. It fell to the ground and exploded
> on impact. His skill and determination were
> characteristic of what he has shown on all
> occasions."

        The personnel of the Force are proud of your son's fine Service record.

        Yours sincerely,

        Minister of National Defence for Air

Knight of the Legion of Honour, April 28th, 2014

Knight of the Legion of Honour, April 28th, 2014

Chapter 17

'The end of one war, the beginning of another.'
– Marcel Croteau

"Marcel, how did the war end for you?"

"I know when the war began for me but defining the end is another story.

"Two months after our last mission and the subsequent screening at the end of our operations, the RAF scrapped all the Halifax aircraft and brought on new Lancasters with a different tour. One of the Lancasters' many attributes were the five caliber machine guns with which they were equipped. With these much bigger bullets than we had used, there was much better capability of defense and attack for the RCAF and RAF. By then, I was finished my tour but I asked to go back into action. To my dismay they told me I'd done enough, a remarkable 39 missions all tolled.

"I went on to be an instructor but I didn't like it and I wasn't a very good communicator. I tried it for a few days and I was working with new trainees. These guys were enthusiastic but had no clue what they were doing or what they would be facing. I felt very uneasy preparing these young guys for a position in the war that for many of them would mean certain death.

"Because I didn't like the role I had been given, I went to my commanding officer and said, 'Send me back on operations or send me home.' He advised me that they had enough replacements now. Therefore, I was advised to go home. This was around November 1944. I didn't know at first where they were going to send me to prepare to leave for home. Eventually, I got posted to Grenoch about 20 miles from Glasgow for about two or three weeks and then we boarded a ship for home in January 1945."

Aircraft VINI VIDI VICHI
"Came, I Saw, I Conquered"

Taking off on last trip
Friday, September 13, 1944
Tholthorpe, Yorkshire, England

"How did that feel leaving the war and coming back home before the war was actually over?"

"It's hard to explain. Having participated in the war effort for almost three years, I was attached to the war and to the outcome. We knew we were winning when so much effort was being put into the war. The American Air Force gave the Luftwaffe a real run for their money. So that really was a boost. They eliminated the Luftwaffe from England and North Africa. One of their tactics was that they didn't paint their aircraft but left them silver so the German fighters wouldn't see them. Also, their gunners were equipped with 50-caliber machine guns. Although the war was undecided as yet, we knew by that time with the Americans involved and the Allied forces in France, the chance of a positive outcome was almost certain."

"I can understand why you might want to be there at the end."

"After you got screened it was very difficult to get back up in the air, especially for the air gunners, who pretty much all had PTSD by then. We were all more than a little crazy, and we were in denial. Our jobs were not like being in the airplane with the other guys who were more or less protected. We were alone and precariously attached behind the airplane. We felt really exposed with the four props screaming all around when flying through the clouds. The propellers turned the air into what looked like little tornadoes (my artistic nature at work)."

"I gather you must have seen all sorts of shapes and forms in the clouds that would be interesting."

"I had to try not to be distracted because I was there to do my job. I got used to it in a way. But the exception was when we were going through storms. The air would circle down like funnels. Encountering these air currents was like hitting a pile of rocks. And the plane would shake and shudder all the way back to the rear turret where the nerve-wracking motion was amplified."

"Most of us cannot imagine being in a situation like that. I find turbulence in an airliner bad enough but you were able to find the courage to carry on and perform the job you were required to do."

"We didn't have a choice. It was do or die. But it also explains one of the lesser reasons we came home in such a poor mental state. There were plenty of reasons for Post-Traumatic Stress Disorder to get its claws into us. I frequently find myself going back to the war even though I physically left it behind a very long time ago. I think this happens because I haven't talked very much about it to anyone. I'm releasing some of the power it has over me right now as I'm talking."

"I hope that's a good thing."

"Yes, it is. For a while there in my mind in our conversation today, I was on the ship coming home and then I went back to the war. It seems that the war never leaves you. That war had to be won, even if we did have to send kids to fight it. Just think if Hitler had been able to invade England. How would we ever have been able to stop him?"

"When will we ever learn?"

Chapter 18

'If you want to be a millionaire,
start with a billion dollars and launch a new airline.'
– Richard Branson

"Have I talked about my airline yet?"

"No, you have not."

"I think I have been avoiding the subject. What I really wanted to do when I came home from the war was not farming, not buying seeds which I did for a very short time, and definitely not selling farm equipment from a non-existent inventory. My dream was to create an airline. When I was in the service, I was promoted by ten ranks. Every time I went up a notch, I received a pay raise and every time I got paid, I sent home one-half of the total amount.

"By the time I returned home after the war, my family had a second farm which my older brother operated. I owned a quarter section of it which I had paid for with earnings I sent home. I used that section of the farm to obtain a mortgage for the airline I dreamed of. With the funding in place, in September of 1946, I took flying lessons from a guy who instructed pilots during the war, not for the RCAF but to fly Cessna T50s for hauling fish that was caught in some of the northern lakes. Those lessons gave me more self-confidence to move forward with my vision.

"By January of 1948, the money I had saved during the war was dwindling, so I was anxious to get my plans for an airline into motion. I phoned my pilot from the RCAF and who had returned home to Magog, Quebec, to tell him of my plans. He agreed to join me and moved out to Alberta. We each invested $2,000 and bought a Hanson 5 with twin 250HP motors for $10,000. Our loan for the plane was $6,000 and in those days, that was a large amount of money. The purchase of the plane began an adventure that was meant to be the fulfillment of a lifelong dream.

"Our plan was to make money hauling cargo. However, our business was fraught with problems. We were very young with no business experience and made a lot of mistakes. A major problem was that we listened to people who were giving us terrible advice including buying the wrong model of airplane. It was not the type of aircraft for what we wanted to do which was to move cargo. It was too big and it was 20 years ahead of its time. First, it was necessary to modify the body for commercial transport before we could use it. Another problem was that sometimes we transported goods to our destination and found we had no cargo to carry with us on our return trip. The plane burned 45 gallons of gas per hour so it was very costly to fly with no cargo.

"We decided we would fly loads of fish from the northern lakes, south. In Bonnyville, we were close to the Saskatchewan border and thought the lakes there were full of fish. In reality, they were empty. We found out too late that the lakes were over fished during the Depression and the war. Before then, in Saskatchewan, the lakes had been fished on a small scale using sleighs and horses for transportation.

"Our license was for cargo weighing up to 2,400 pounds which was the amount the plane was rated to carry. That was not much of a load for a twin-engine plane because the maximum weight included the weight of the pilots, the gas and a barrel of oil which meant we could carry only 1,500 pounds of freight. We needed to be able to carry up to 6,000 pounds in order to cover our expenses and make a profit. However, when we carried that size of a load, it felt like we were pushing the air as we flew and the tail seemed a little heavy!!!

After the War, CNL (Croteau & Lacaille) Airlines operated out of Cole Lake, Alberta 1947-1948

"It was suggested to us that we might try flying with a cargo of furs from Saskatchewan to Alberta. There was a law in Saskatchewan that a trapper could have only so many beaver and muskrat pelts. Because there was an abundance of muskrat at the time, a guy came to us and suggested we find a buyer in Alberta with a license to buy fur pelts from Saskatchewan. He said we could make lots of money flying the furs to Alberta. We were just desperate enough to give it a try. By then, we had been in business for three months and needed to make some money. We had payments to make. The fur buyer we had lined up warned us to be careful and not get caught transporting furs without a license. The rules were very strict and it would tarnish our reputations. The outpost where he was located was about 12 miles north of Bonnyville.

"On Good Friday, April 3, 1948, having returned to Bonnyville after a trip delivering cargo, our plane was sitting on a nearby frozen lake. In winter, the plane was equipped with skis. After landing, the skis were hot and they melted everything they came in contact with, which in this case was the ice the plane had landed on. The result was that after stopping, the plane would freeze to the surface of the lake. In order to fly our cargo to Saskatchewan in -20° Celsius weather the skis had to be disengaged from the ice that was holding them to the surface of the lake. It was my job to do this. I had to hold onto the end of each of the wings and rock the plane to loosen the skis from the ice. Then, I ran along the side of the plane while the pilot taxied over the ice, opened the doors, and jumped into the plane. I was worried about the danger and potential for injuries but the pilot remained oblivious to my concerns. He should have taxied around in circles to melt the ice off the skis before taking off. However, he did not want to do so, as we did not have a lot of gas. I thought it would be better to gas the plane and leave the next day. We only had a flight of 15 miles to get to our destination, so my pilot decided we had enough gas to get there, he just kept going and took off. I told him to turn back because I was sure we would not make it. He rarely listened to what I had to say. He hit some trees as he tried to gain altitude and the blades of one of the propellers were broken. I directed the three guys in the back of the fuselage to get on the floor between the wing spars to prepare for a crash landing.

"The motor started vibrating and shaking horribly until it cut out and down we went. When we were taking off, I saw the fence ahead of us along which the farmer had placed rocks. The plane went down with a bang, caught the fence, and dragged 30 yards of it along behind us attached to the tail of the airplane. Ahead of us, we spotted two very large stacks of straw with greenery in between. There had been a lot of snow over the winter and it had piled up on the vegetation. We hit the ground and started sliding toward the mound. Our pilot had no control over the plane because in addition to our motor problems, one of our wings was missing 20 feet. The plane continued on its trajectory into the straw and snow which luckily softened the impact. Fortunately, none of us were seriously injured when the undercarriage was ripped off. A ski tore off and came through the fuselage between the spars that supported the wings. The three guys, one of who was my brother-in-law, were still lying down in the back as we crashed. The ski hit one guy on the hip as it passed between two of the passengers. It cut him but not seriously. We all walked out of the plane, me with a sore knee and the pilot with a bump on his head. Too bad hitting his head didn't knock some sense into him. All this happened just because the pilot would not turn around to get more gas."

"Well, I guess the good news is there were no serious injuries resulting from the crash."

"The bad news is that we had no money left. We had only been in business for three months. It had cost a lot of money not only to buy the aircraft but to start up a new business which required the purchase of the requisite licenses and other expenses. With no cash reserves, it was pretty gloomy to think about starting up our business all over again.

"Optimistically, because the plane was insured, we decided to give our airline another try, notwithstanding our concerns over money. It took until August to get a replacement aircraft. We managed to revive our cargo business which went well for a few months before the pilot made another foolish error and the plane crashed into the ice on the lake near Bonnyville December 11, 1948. There was a snow squall and the pilot could not see the surface of the lake on which he planned to land. He landed anyway only to find there was not enough ice to support the plane and it partially sank into the water. We had to thaw out the plane before we could remove it from the lake which took until December 23. It took another ten days to patch it up. The plane had to be examined and approved to be flight worthy by the authorities in Edmonton. They condemned the plane to my great disappointment. In fact, I was devastated. Thankfully, again, no one was injured in the crash but that was the end of my dream.

In the Cockpit

"I lost everything when the second plane crashed. I was completely devastated by the loss. I had worked extremely hard for most of my life and particularly so to create an airline. That was probably the lowest point in my life. After all, I had a growing family to support. Both of the crashes were because of pilot error. He was the pilot of my crew during the war, so I knew he was very capable, and in fact, was an excellent pilot. Unfortunately, he liked to take chances. I depended on him because he had a pilot's license. I had taken flying lessons but found that just as I needed to prepare for a landing, I would blank out for a few seconds. I lost confidence in my abilities. I'm sure it was a symptom of PTSD.

"My pilot and I had a lot of problems communicating with one another. I tended to be more cautious while he was more tuned in to flying by the seat of his pants. For example, during the war, the bombers landed at the airports at a speed of 100 miles per hour. Where he and I were hauling cargo, the plane needed to be slowed down to 70 miles per hour before landing. My pilot acted as if he were flying a bomber and landed at a speed which was much too fast for the lakes we used as runways. When we bought the first plane, we were given a demonstration of how to land the aircraft. The flying instructor demonstrated slowing the plane down to a landing speed of 70 mph by lowering the flaps to create some drag. Unfortunately, my pilot was not present for the demonstration. I think I made a bad choice for a pilot for a commercial enterprise such as I was trying to create. This fiasco taught me the importance of finding the right partner in business."

"What happened to your pilot after the loss of your airline?"

"Much later, I ran into him at the Victoria Flying Club on Vancouver Island where I kept my plane I owned at the time. He worked a few jobs after our airline disaster and then joined the armed forces again and was stationed at Cold Lake, Alberta. I heard that he had quite a reputation. His rank was flight lieutenant but he was still a risk taker. Whenever he landed at the base with leaves and branches in the undercarriage of his plane, he was demoted to Flight Officer. Then, he would gain a promotion back to Flight Lieutenant which he maintained until he landed again with leaves and branches in the undercarriage precipitating yet another demotion. That seemed to be an established cycle for him. It was rumored that he liked to kill foxes with his wingtips, but I hoped that was a gross exaggeration."

Marcel balancing a propeller on a CNL aircraft after damage from ice

The Crew

Chapter 19

'It is important to look forward, not behind.'
– Marcel Croteau

"*I cannot imagine how difficult it must have been for you to lose your dream of creating an airline.*"

"It was a devastating experience for me. However, I believe that it is through experiencing hardship and disappointment that one can fully appreciate the lightness of life. From my childhood on, I was a very serious guy in many ways and my war experience only amplified my rather grim outlook on life. However, there were a few occasions when I let loose. For example, some of my buddies and I were in a bar one night shortly after the French General De Gaulle (leader of Free France 1940–1942, head of the French Provisional Government 1944–1946, and French President 1959–1969) came to Quebec for a visit. We stood on top of some tables and gave a rather raucous rendition of De Gaulle's controversial speech ending with '*Vive le* France. *Vive le* Quebec *Libre.*'"

"*You seem to me to have been able to counterbalance your serious side with a wicked sense of humor and a positive outlook on life.*"

"That is true now, but in the past, I was different. When I came home from the war, I immediately got married; and a short time later, we started our family. I felt the weight of my responsibilities and needed to find work in order to support my family. After the demise of my airline, I went to Yellowknife where I worked in a mine for a few months. Working there was quite unpleasant and the wages were no better than in 'civilization.' They charged us for room and board, and there were deductions from the company's store for any purchases we made. I could only work there for so long before I found being underground too much of a trial. Some guys spent their entire lives working underground, but I grew up on the prairies and spent a good part of my days outside and was not suited to working so far under the earth where it was so dark and dirty.

"It was an opportunity, though, to meet an interesting guy from England. His name was Tony. Apparently, he had quite a history before coming to Canada, although, he did not share the details with me. He was younger than me and had been a commando during the war. He was a good-looking man and he showed me why. He was carrying a picture of himself in his wallet that was taken before he had a nose job done. The surgery really changed his looks because the nose he was born with was huge and dominated his face. He said his nose had given him an inferiority complex which I did not question. There were three of us, including Tony, who became friends while working for the Consolidating Mining and Smelting Company. Tony was afraid of ghosts which we found out during a conversation about the ghosts that were present in the mine. Tony was preoccupied with ghosts and told us they were the spirits of miners who had lost their lives in the underground mine.

"Each day, we entered the mine by going down the shaft to the floor of the mine. We walked about a mile and a half until we reached our work area. At the end of the day, we climbed ladders to get out of the mine. One night, the third guy and I decided to leave Tony where he was because he had not yet finished his work, and we were ready to leave for the day. We climbed about two thirds up the ladder, stopped our ascent, and started to moan, hoping the noises sounded ghostly. Tony came out of the tunnel where he was working and flashed his light on. He was clearly agitated and ran around like a chicken with its head cut off for about ten minutes. Finally, we let him know it was just us making the noises."

"Was he angry at you for tricking him?"

"Oh, no, he took it well. He was planning to leave soon to go to the Nahanni Valley where according to a number of stories circulating around, there was a lot of gold to be found. Tony was a very likeable guy, a dreamer who was obsessed with gold, so we called him Nahanni Tony. The thought of gold was intoxicating. I would have gone with him but because I had a family, I decided not to. Which was a good choice for me because he never found any gold when he was there. He came back and took a job working in a giant gold mine. I knew he was fixated on gold so I was not surprised when I read in the newspaper that he had stolen a brick of gold from the mine where he was working. Apparently, after the theft, he went to Vancouver where he boarded a ship for Australia. When the ship arrived in Australia officials boarded it, arrested him, and sent him to jail. That was the last I heard of him.

"I had arrived in Yellowknife in early summer but by the end of October I could not stand working underground any longer. For a while, I worked for a company building sewer lines. We dug the trenches by hand through the permafrost. A guy I worked with who must have been at least seven feet tall sat on top of a backhoe for most of the day, occasionally screaming orders at us. When we dug, we had to wait for the permafrost to melt in order to be able to dig deeper. It was mostly sand.

"The job was not interesting enough to hold me there, so I got a job working for Northern Gateways. A train brought supplies up from Fort McMurray which were then to be transported on the Mackenzie River to the Arctic. It was my job to load dynamite onto a barge attached to a tugboat that hauled the load to Fort McPherson. I was also one of the crew members on the tugboat and traveled as far as Fort Ray before I had to leave. When I had been digging for the sewer installation, I had a minor accident. Sometimes, we had to break up rocks with sledgehammers. Just before I left for my new job, a piece of rock flew at my chest causing an injury. On the trip across Great Slave Lake to Fort Rae, there was a lot of work to do on the tugboat so I wasn't paying attention to my injury. By the time we arrived at our destination, my wound was badly infected.

"Fort Rae was an interesting place. The Dogrib (now known as the Tlicho) and the Yellowknife aboriginals of the Dene Nation, lived there. There was also an RCMP post. Luckily for me, there also was a hospital which was run by the Grey Nuns. A distant relative of my father who was a Grey Nun in Quebec had acted as the architect for the building of the Order's hospitals in Quebec in 1738. I also had cousins who were Grey Nuns. Naturally, I mentioned this to the nuns when I arrived at the hospital for treatment. There was no doctor available when I was there so the nuns put on their 'kid gloves' and took care of me as if I were royalty. I spent three days in the hospital but they never charged me for my care. By the time I was ready to leave, there was an RCMP plane scheduled to arrive in Fort Rae to pick up two RCMP officers and transport them to Yellowknife. I managed to catch a ride with them but it cost me my last dollar, a total of $70.

"Back in Yellowknife, I needed to make some money so that I could buy a flight home to Bonnyville where my family was living and also to send money to my wife. I managed to secure a job working as a 'flunkie' in the kitchen of a cafeteria. My workday started at 5 a.m. It was my job to set up the cafeteria for breakfast and then do the cleanup. I usually went for a nap afterward and returned around 10 a.m. to get ready for lunch. It was a tedious job with no merits. Miners, who were very tough and aggressive, were our customers. They came after their shifts were done and used all of the available tables. If they sat in one area all together, it would have cut my work in half. I asked them to fill up the large tables they were using before moving on to more of them. I stood there watching them to see what they would do. One smart aleck went over to a large empty table for ten and sat down by himself. His belligerence annoyed me, so I walked over to him, grabbed him, picked him up and moved him to join others at a table, and sat him down. The guy was so surprised, his skin blanched to white. That poor miner always sat with the others after his encounter with me. The other 'flunkies' were very proud of me that I had put the guy in his place! I did not stay much longer. As soon as I had enough money, I left and went home. That was in 1950.

"At home, I worked for the next few months as a bouncer and bartender in my father-in-law's new business venture which was a partnership in a new hotel. I had trained in wrestling when I was still in school and was very strong so I think he thought I could do the job. I worked in the bar early in the day but when the lumber camps closed for the night, guys would come in and get drunk and rowdy. Fights would break out every night, and it was my job to stop them. One night, two WWII veterans came in and got into a fight. They were big guys, but I grabbed them and tossed them out into the street. My wrestling ability came in handy more than once. I spent six weeks in the Midlands during our training in the UK, taking a commando course for hand-to-hand combat. The techniques I learned helped me to control my actions in physical conflicts so that I didn't hurt anyone if I didn't have to. I was really strong. Besides that, bullies are usually cowards.

"On one occasion, when I was about 30, a guy from Bonnyville came to me and offered to pay me $500 to beat up someone for him. Of course, I declined. I had no issue with the intended victim. Besides, I never hurt anyone. When there was a bully involved, I would teach him a lesson, but it was more about scaring him than doing any physical harm.

"One night, when I was stationed in York during the war, I was walking along the street past a pub when some guys who had been drinking triple gins came out the door. They were heading across the street to a building that was the source of a lot of noise. There was a bobby standing on the corner and so I asked him what was going on? He told me there was a dance happening above the church. I thought I would go and investigate. Within two minutes of my arrival, the eight drunk army guys I had seen earlier, started beating up a lance corporal from Owl Squadron 420. I jumped in and started pulling the guys off the airman and tossed them two at a time down the stairs. Unfortunately, the stairs were lined with more guys who got caught up with the drunks resulting in a melee of arms and legs as they rolled down the stairs. I left by gingerly stepping over the bodies and headed out the door. To my surprise, there was an MP standing on the street outside the door. Fighting was not allowed among the enlisted, so I was sure I was in big trouble. However, to my great relief, the MP's only remark to me was 'move along, son' which I quickly did. Perhaps, I saved him the trouble of breaking up the fight.

"After I returned home from Yellowknife, I took a job with Mutual of Omaha, an insurance company that provided life and accident insurance. Up until then, there was no medical insurance available for anyone. This was in the early 1950s. I decided to give insurance sales a try when the insurance company added medical insurance. For about one year, April to the following March, I went door to door, farm to farm throughout my community. My car was a 1947 Ford deluxe coupe. There were no snowplows in those days so when there was a snowstorm, most people stayed home. One day, after a storm, I knocked on the door of a potential customer. He had some friends visiting with him. When they opened the door, they asked me where my horse was. I told them I came by car (there were no snow tires in those days) which they did not believe until I showed it to them. I had used the clutch and low gears and drove only 4 to 5 mph to get there. Those guys became customers because they admired my dedication and determination. In that year, I sold over 400 policies for which I have a certificate for membership in Mutual of Omaha 400 Club. By then, just about everyone in the community and surrounding area had purchased health insurance, so I had very few potential customers left. Another problem was that Tommy Douglas was elected in Saskatchewan and created Canada's universal health care system."

"It's very impressive that someone as quiet and shy as you are was able to make those cold calls that led to all those sales."

"When I put my mind to do something, I do it. However, every time I knocked on the door, I felt that pain in my abdomen that I carry everywhere I go."

"Were you living in Bonneville when selling insurance?"

"Yes. I was back to where I started. By leaving Bonnyville temporarily, I had acquired some work experience but not in any field in which I was interested in making a career. I look back and think that if my father had not pulled me out of school to work on the farm, I think my life would have been quite different. I can see that I wasted some of my life. I could have become someone else."

"On the other hand, those negative experiences helped you to become the person that you are today because of what you learned from them."

"I overcame my situation as best as I could. At that time, if you didn't have a high school education, many employers were not going to hire you. I was still feeling like there was a black cloud hanging over me."

"Does that dark cloud represent frustration at not able to do what you wanted and use your full potential?"

"It does. I was living in a small town where there was a lot of judgment and criticism. I felt persecuted. Some people were against insurance salesmen, an attitude that spilled over into anybody who wore a white collar and a tie. And as always, there was the elephant in the room, my PTSD. I had a short fuse which meant I had a low tolerance for the bad behavior of others."

"How long did you live in Bonnyville?"

"Too long. I decided that I would try selling real estate. There were real estate offices everywhere so there was stiff competition for sales. It was difficult to survive in that environment. I was a commissioner of oaths and drew up contracts for purchase and sale plus mortgages. I didn't have any training, I just drew them up using my own devices and none of my mortgages were ever refused by the administration offices or the land registry office. I learned that all in my higher education of grade 9!!!"

"Well, you were a very resourceful guy and a quick study. Did you sell real estate as well?"

"Yes, I did, but it was a small town. I only had a couple deals a year. There were too many of us chasing too few sales. It was a difficult time in that summer of 1960. It was particularly difficult for me because there was no real estate moving at all. The economy had just taken a nosedive and nobody was buying anything for about three months. It seemed like the economy was doing a little better in Edmonton, and there was much more inventory to sell, so I decided to move there. In Edmonton, I got a job with a real estate company that had units for sale in the high rise called the McLeod building. It is the last remaining building in Edmonton which is an example of the commercial and residential architecture of the Chicago Style. My new employer gave me a $120 a week draw when sales were good, but sometimes as much as $500 a week if sales were better. It may not seem like much today, but it was a lot of money in those days when wages were less than twenty dollars a day. The wages were good but once again PTSD reared its ugly head. I spent a few months trying to work for other people but once again I found it very difficult. I blamed myself and thought there was something wrong with me but I had no idea what it was. So that was my life with PTSD. I felt there was a duality in my personality. Part of it came from the way that my father and my older sister and brother treated me when I was a child. According to them, I was no good. There was one side of my personality that agreed with them and then there was the other side that knew better. A constant conflict in my mind was carrying on as I coped with the opposing viewpoints. That was the negative part of my life, but it had a big influence on me and those around me.

"After my stint as a real estate agent in Edmonton, I moved with my family back to Bonnyville. There was raw land available there and so I bought a parcel and proposed a subdivision. I went to the town council with a plan that I would sell ten houses. I then talked to the owner of the property and he agreed to sell to me after I explained to him that I wanted to build ten houses. The subdivision was subject to pre-selling those ten houses. The Mayor bought two homes which were a duplex. One day, I sold four houses and within a week, I had sold all of them. It seemed everybody wanted a new house. This was in 1962. That was the beginning of changing the town into a place of more modern houses. My plans for houses were different from those built in the twenties and thirties. Although the houses were small, they were desirable because of their affordability and because they had a bathroom. When I first started building in Bonnyville, the three-bedroom houses had 1,200 ft.^{2} and the two-bedroom houses were about 950 ft.^{2}. The 1,200 ft.^{2} house sold at \$12,000, and the two-bedroom homes sold for \$7,200. None of them still exist."

"So that got you started in property development."

"That career really started when I was in Edmonton. I watched what they were doing there so I brought the idea with me. I didn't do the actual construction. I had contractors and I sold to them and they paid me a commission which was \$500 or more per house. I made as much as \$15,000 for my commissions and I acquired one of the new houses for my growing family."

"That was a good move on your part. You had a vision and you made it happen."

"There was not much left for me to do in Bonnyville after I sold the subdivision, so I left my family there while I moved on to British Columbia. I moved into a motel room in Coquitlam while I looked for work. There did not seem to be anything in real estate that was appealing. I then went to Vancouver where I found a couple of possibilities. I had two interviews and got the job offered in the second interview as an estimator for steel bridges and buildings. I had to estimate the numbers of every piece of steel and every bolt and absolutely everything that goes into building a structure. They gave me the blueprints and from them, I estimated every piece of steel required for construction. I had to learn all the names of every single plate or hanger or screw or bolt. A mistake would be costly."

"Did you have any related experience for this job?"

"Well, I did some estimating with houses to figure out the cost of the building materials but it wasn't the same. One of my projects was the CN Bridge which is next to the second Narrows Bridge in Vancouver. I also prepared estimates for buildings and factories in the Middle East. The parent company was in England and had projects worldwide.

"The work went well, but my relationship with the employees was very difficult and I remained for about six months. I would have stayed longer but I just wasn't accepted by the group. I was not a big city guy and there was some prejudice against me being French Canadian. Some of the employees came back at night to check my work and the next day, accused me of making a mistake. I talked to the manager who said he was happy with my work. 'You know,' he said, 'you work very hard, and I can appreciate your feelings.' It

189

seemed like it was a bit of a defeat, but I felt I had done a pretty good job.

"PTSD was unknown at the time but nevertheless, it was most likely the source of my emotional problems and my difficulties with my employment. My nerves were just shot. I went to the doctor, and he gave me a letter to give to the Department of Veteran Affairs, but I never presented it to the DVA because I had been turned down every time I had appealed to them for help. I still have the letter which says I have a nervous condition. The doctor prescribed pills for me to take.

"I was now in the position of needing another job. I knew how to do steam fitting because I had worked briefly for Texaco at a refinery in Edmonton. Before that, I had done some gas fitting in Bonnyville which is where I acquired pipefitting skills. I joined the union and then secured a job working as a steamfitter in Powell River, north of Vancouver on the Sunshine Coast. We were all members of the union. By then, I was skilled at reading blueprints. I was given a blueprint for just the area we were working on and I started checking on what we were doing. The workers were doing everything backward so that they could make the job last longer. The engineer for the project came to the site and said, 'You've been working on this for a few days. The job should be done by now. What is going wrong?' I explained to him what was slowing down our progress. He said, 'Oh that's good to know.' And he put a whole bunch of guys on notice. Some of us had been working out in the rain from January to March. I became ill and had to stop working.

"Back in Vancouver, I called a guy I knew whose name was Guy Le Fleur (not the hockey player). He was a real estate agent. I met him when I bought my first house in Vancouver, well actually in Coquitlam. He had been in World War II and had lost a leg. We had a lot in common and became good friends. Also we worked well together. Because I found a job in real estate sales in Vancouver, I did not return to the steam-fitting job. I worked with Guy Lefleur for a couple of years. There were two subdivisions with houses that needed to be sold, and I sold them very fast. However, the real estate market tended to go up and down, and we soon found ourselves in a slump where there were no more sales. That was in the '60s in Vancouver. At the time, we were living in a house I bought from Guy Le Fleur when I first moved to Coquitlam and didn't have much money. The house had been repossessed from its owners. I was able to buy it just by taking over the mortgage payments and paying my friend Guy a commission. We lived in that house until 1969 when we moved to Victoria.

"I was pretty lost and was having a lot of problems. I took on another steam-fitting job on the west coast of Vancouver Island at a pulp mill in Gold River. I left my home in Coquitlam on Sunday nights to take the ferry across to Schwartz Bay just north of Victoria. There was a guy from Vancouver with a station wagon who drove me and a few other guys we worked with. The Ford station wagon we rode in had a major leak in the exhaust system and because I sat in the back, I was almost overcome by the carbon monoxide fumes. It was a good thing our road trip wasn't any longer. As it was, I could hardly climb the stairs from the car deck to the passenger deck of the ferry. After disembarking the ferry, we drove to the pulp mill where we spent our days working in the rain. It was a German company that had the contract to build the pulp mill so most of the workers were Germans. I made the mistake of sharing that I had been in the war. That did not go over well them, and they burned whatever of my possessions they could get their hands on as frequently as possible. I had to pay to keep replacing my things so I quit."

"You have been the brunt of an unbelievable amount of bullying in your life."

"I don't like bullies but I've tried to not let them have too much influence on me. I have had a lot of experience in that regard!

"Later on, I moved to Victoria with my family after selling our house in Coquitlam. I'd looked around quite a bit for another job but I didn't have much confidence in myself. I eventually found employment working for a building contractor. I worked on the roof of the house we were building where it was quite unsafe because I didn't have proper footwear. My feet hurt because I was wearing leather shoes, and it was slippery up there. Gables were planned for the roof and I had never built anything like that before. There was a rough drawing, and I think it was sent as an afterthought. It wasn't a functional plan but having learned to read blueprints I worked it out.

"After moving to Sydney, I occasionally went to the Legion to drink a beer with the V 33 Navy squadron. It was the coastal combat squadron which monitored Russian submarine activity. There, I met some Air Force guys who had bought starter homes in a subdivision for about $17,000. Some of them stayed in those homes for 20 years and subsequently sold them for $300,000. At the time, the lots they were buying were very cheap. So I made an offer on a lot and I negotiated the option of buying the remaining lots in the subdivision. All I had was $100 down but I knew the procedures for the process. Therefore, I was successful in securing the properties. The next step was to draw some house plans. They were two bedroom homes with a basement that could be finished for more living space. The exteriors were stucco and they all looked more or less the same. They all sold quickly. Two of my sons, Guy and George, were in their early 20s by then. They both had a lot of sense and skill in the construction trade so they joined me to get these houses built."

"A chip off the old block?"

"Perhaps, but their mother was creative and very sensible too. The boys have done very well and they are still building homes. I was happy to bring them into the company. They had both worked at framing for other builders so they knew what they were doing. My sons worked really fast and built economically. Therefore, they produced a good saleable product. Together we built more than 350 houses on Vancouver Island.

"We also built a manufacturing plant for trusses with very little knowledge of the business. My son designed the equipment that was required and we set up production. When the oil business came to northeastern Alberta, I went there to have a look around. The result was that I went into partnership with a guy who had an existing truss manufacturing plant near Edmonton. We moved back to Alberta, and I eventually bought out my partner. The business still continues to be operated by the family."

"Well, you probably will never think that you led a boring life."

"My life has always been filled with adventures and new experiences for me. In a way, it's been a problem though. I have never been able to stay in one place for long. It has never been about the money, it's been about the accomplishment. Building starter homes to help people that needed affordable housing gave me a sense of satisfaction. I think that came from my conditioning while living through the Depression. I was always happy to help someone obtain a new home. It wasn't about building a big fancy house that a rich person would live in. I still remember my first lawyer in Victoria. He was married to one of the Woodward girls (the Woodward Department Store in downtown Vancouver has since been converted into condos and geared to income housing). He was well known and held in high esteem. One day, he came to the site to look at the houses I was building and saw that they were starter homes. He thought that I was building great big mansions. I told him I wasn't married to a Woodward girl! He was a very nice person. During the war, he was a captain and was about 20 years older than me. He was an Englishman and very refined, much better than I was used to. I learned a lot from him."

Chapter 20

'Success is not final, failure is not fatal.
It is the courage to continue that counts.'
– Winston Churchill

"Early on in our conversations, you described to me the first part of your mid-air collision but we did not finish the story. What was the outcome of that terrifying event?"

"We were following through on our decision not to bail out but to try and make it back to England after bombing our target. Because of the damage to the plane, the journey home was very eventful. The aircraft kept lurching and shuddering because the damaged engine was partly engaged in a stall mode. Daybreak was coming which was another danger we faced because it increased our visibility. An enemy night jet fighter crossed above our path at about 8,000 feet. Luckily he did not see us as we were flying about 5,000 feet below him. We held our collective breath as it passed over us because we were not equipped to fight in daylight. My machine guns didn't have the range for daylight air-to-air combat and our aircraft was not maneuverable for evasive action due to the damage from the collision.

"With that danger behind us, we passed the French Coast at approximately 6,500 feet when the enemy's light anti-aircraft defenses opened fire on us. There were explosions happening all around us. Some of the flak from the explosions hit the aircraft. The pilot had to quickly put the nose down to get more speed. Fortunately, we were successful in getting out of their range without receiving too much damage.

"After safely crossing the channel to England, the aircraft was a bit more stable. The bombs that we were no longer carrying and the fuel we had used were half the total weight on taking off. This reduction in weight decreased some of the danger we might encounter when we tried to land. Our flying altitude was too low for us to bail out, giving us no other choice than to come in and attempt a landing. However, by the time we got to Yorkshire the report from the flight engineer indicated that we were almost out of fuel. The pilot called Mayday and was given clearance to land immediately. The tension in the air was palpable. When the pilot advised us to get into a position for a crash landing, I was still at my position in the turret. I needed to quickly leave the turret and join the others in the fuselage. We assumed the crash position between the wing spars. I barely got there before our pilot came in over the runway flying much too fast for a safe landing. His only option was to shut down the motors to reduce the speed. When we landed, our right wing hit the runway, and the aircraft ground to a stop. I was thrown around the inside of the plane as were the others. Once we got our equilibrium, we all piled out through the emergency exit and saw that ambulances were all around us, waiting to give us assistance should we have required it. Luckily, the aircraft was almost out of fuel and so did not explode or catch fire on impact with the ground. The ambulance attendants checked us out. I was so happy to be on the ground and alive that the trauma and injuries didn't seem important. Anyhow, the adrenaline was still flowing. We were all shaken very badly but were so grateful to be alive that we hugged each other all the while laughing hysterically, especially when we saw the damage to the plane. The tail section was demolished, and the rear turret was resting on the airfield away from the aircraft. It was then that I realized what a close call I had because I almost didn't get out of the turret in time. My nose was bleeding and when asked about it I said, 'It's just a nosebleed.' As it turned out, my nose was broken which only came to light after the swelling went down a few days later. My back was injured and bruised which I also didn't complain about at the time. Culturally, in those days, one didn't complain. Besides, our injuries seemed like a minor detail after what we had been through.

"Two days later, we all had to go up again in another aircraft. The pilot was made to practice taking off and landing three times. I think this action was meant to be something like getting back on a bicycle after falling off. All members of the crew had to be in attendance on these flights. Our pilot was awarded the 'Distinguished Medal for Flying' for his perseverance and determination while: flying the aircraft through adverse conditions for flying with an unmanageable aircraft while continuing to fly through enemy fire and getting a direct hit on the target and (most important from my point of view) returning to home base with all members of his crew."

Chapter 21

'There are two types of casualties of war: those that are killed in action and those that are killed from alcohol and prescription drug use after the war.'
– Marcel Croteau

"After the war, did you make any connections with other members of your crew?"

"Although I tried to keep in contact with my flying mates in Bomber Command, I had not seen anyone from my squadron since the war except for my pilot. As you know, we had an airline together after the war and that partnership did not work out.

"When I made attempts to find some of my crew, it became quite a depressing endeavor. My son played hockey for the junior teams and he had a tournament in Thunder Bay where my friend the wireless operator lived. While there, I found out he had died in 1962 from a heart attack. By 1966, four of the crew had died of heart attacks and alcoholism. Those guys were all from Quebec. I lost touch with them after the war and never saw them again. They were not my close friends even though we had spent hours together on our missions.

"I continue to be very good friends with my navigator's family but I never did see him again after the war. He died ten days before I was able to track down his family. In 1992, when

I moved to Montreal, I searched for him. I looked everywhere but I had difficulty finding him because in Quebec, women keep their surnames and I did not know his wife's name. Everything was in her name because my friend gambled heavily and lost two houses. My navigator earned big wages because he was a really savvy, highly intelligent man. Although he was making a lot of money, he was gambling it away, drinking excessively, and showing signs of doing drugs as well. His wife had two jobs in order to feed the family but she was still having difficulty providing for the children. I suspect he too had PTSD as a result of severe emotional trauma from his participation in the war.

"I could tell when I looked at other veterans of the war that they had not received the help that I eventually received. We were all casualties of the war. It was not recognized at the time but there were very real but invisible consequences of the war. When I came home from the war, I went to the DVA (Department of Veterans Affairs) and they said to me, 'What are you doing here? You look okay to me. Go home.' Of course, I looked normal so I must be normal.

"The war had ended but the emotions created by the effects of the trauma we experienced lived on. The negative emotions, the PTSD, and the fears were so destructive. I feared the world because those in it became the enemy. When I had difficulties with day-to-day living, it made my symptoms worse. When I was having problems, I was afraid to leave the house and I was very depressed. I questioned everything about myself. Messages that I was 'no good' or that I was 'not good enough' rang in my head, mimicking messages I constantly heard in my childhood. Looking back, I may have had a certain amount of PTSD even as a child.

"When I was fighting in the war, I had to concentrate on what I was doing. It had been my habit to sweep everything under the carpet so that nothing interfered with the experience of the moment. I didn't allow my emotions to come to the surface. But when I came home and was in a safe place, I started having problems. I had these attacks where you have to blow in a paper bag to get your breathing back to normal. At the time, they called it hyperventilation but now it's recognized as a symptom of a panic attack. When I was in the real estate business, at one point the market went flat. I had a family to support and payments to make. I started having panic attacks, and the doctor gave me some little pills, but they didn't help. Nobody understood the problem at that time. I went to a psychiatrist, and he prescribed me a bunch of sugar pills. I guess he figured I was just imagining things. That was in the late '50s. I was very strong physically and even at my age now, 95, I am still strong. I have a strong constitution and good genes. In fact, my doctor says that I have the body of a 65-year-old so physically I'm well, but emotionally, maybe not so much!!!"

"I think you are remarkable!"

"At the time, it seemed like there was no avenue for my recovery from this invisible affliction that affected my mind, not my body. It was like living under a dark cloud and the only thing that was a band-aid for my problems seemed to be alcohol. But the alcohol took me back in time to the war when I went to sleep so that was not a very good solution. It took over 60 years to get help. Most of my crewmembers had died by then and they never did get any help.

"I now live alone and I can decide what to do and what to eat and what to do for myself. I know that I have had to be resilient to survive. I learned that very early in life. I have always managed to bounce back from adversity. But not without a cost to myself and others. After the war, I would go right to hell but I would eventually climb out of it even though the depression was relentless. I just couldn't see anything that was positive and I was afraid to talk about myself to anyone. I didn't talk about my war experience because most of the people I spent time with then were 'zombies' (draft dodgers), and it didn't seem appropriate. I tried to repress all those terrible experiences. Going to bed at night, I would say to myself that tomorrow I'm going to do this or that but I would get up the next day and it was like the day was stormy even though the sunshine was beautiful. I didn't want to go out and face the world. However, over the years, I've learned to handle the depression and it doesn't bother me much anymore. Of course, I have really worked on my emotional health through therapy and taking self-development courses for 15 years. That's where all my money went. I studied in California and Montreal but I never talked about the war. I hid that under the carpet. If I had talked about it then, I think I might have become healthier sooner.

"My experience working as an estimator for a steel company in Vancouver is a very good example of how I struggled with my emotional problems in the workplace. I was having a really difficult time and was not able to find any help.

"For me, the underlying challenge of having PTSD was not knowing what was wrong with me. I had so much depression that I tried to hide. Now that they understand PTSD, and I've had treatment, I can go back to these moods that I had and think about how awful it all was. I know one night I was thinking, not too seriously but seriously enough, about taking my airplane up and crashing it. After surviving all my dangerous missions overseas, I never expected that when I came home I would be contemplating taking my own life. Thankfully, I'm still here but at the time I thought, 'Why am I thinking like this?' We didn't know about PTSD then. I thought there must be something wrong with me and of course, there was.

"When I was assessed by the DVA, and they heard the account of my mid-air collision they didn't believe me. I phoned a fellow I knew who was there at the airfield when we landed and he wrote a letter to the DVA that he had seen the airplane with the damage and everything else on that day. It was very difficult to get support, financial or emotional, at the DVA. It seemed like they were there to save money. Coming back from the war, we needed a lot of assistance, but there was not the help we needed available. We had been told in England to go home and get married. When I sent my doctor's reports to the DVA, they were lost. After a lot of persistence, I was able to get some assistance. But it took a very long time and I had to get very angry. Finally, I phoned my Member of Parliament, contacted the newspaper, and hired a lawyer.

"In the past when I went to the grocery store, I had to carefully figure out if I had enough money to buy what I needed. After my long battle with the DVA, I finally received some compensation for my PTSD which now allows me to live comfortably. It made a huge difference for me. I have enough to live on now. Now, I don't have to worry, but it took the DVA 63 years to recognize that I had PTSD."

Chapter 22

'In the air force, they say the two most beautiful things
in the world are airplanes and women.
But actually, I really think ladies come first.'
– Marcel Croteau

*"I can tell from your stories that you have always enjoyed the
company of ladies."*

"It is true that I have had a number of girlfriends over the
years when I was single. In my teens, I usually had a girlfriend.
The girls I dated were Roman Catholic French Canadians
which meant they were raised with strict rules. As a result, they
were 'good girls.' They were also very shy. I was too and was
not very socially developed. By the time I was 19, I was
wearing an Air Force uniform which did seem to attract the
ladies. When we were in training in Canada, our curfew was 9
p.m. So there wasn't much romance in Canada, well hardly
any. After I arrived in England, I found the ladies to be very
friendly and engaging so I was able to further develop my
social skills. Generally, I was open to learning and felt like a
sponge wanting to absorb everything. We met many of the
English girls at local dances and pubs where we bought them
drinks. We also had dances in the mess halls on our base where
we got to know the enlisted ladies (WAFs). If I did not have a

girlfriend at home, I might have married one of the English girls. Many of them were keen to move to Canada.

"When I returned home after the war, I immediately married my girlfriend, and we spent 36 years together raising our family. By 1980, I was really struggling with myself, my relationship with my wife, and my business interests. My sons and I had built a large number of houses and were operating two truss factories. We had created all of that and the stress of trying to be on top of everything was getting to me. Although I never drank at the office, I found myself going out for lunch where I would have a couple of triple ryes. Later scotch became my drink of choice. Alcohol seemed to make my life easier to bear because it calmed down my PTSD symptoms. Eventually, I was consuming a bottle of scotch a day and my evenings at home were spent drinking. I had a budgie bird who used to sit on my eyeglasses and sip from my glass of scotch as I took a sip. I can truly say I never drank alone. But I was definitely on a downward spiral.

"One day, I had enough and decided to end my relationship with alcohol. I stopped drinking and joined Alcoholics Anonymous. I attended meetings regularly for about three months. At one of the meetings, the leader came to me and suggested that I did not belong in the AA group and I should consider joining a group called the EST Training. I decided to give it a try. I went to my first meeting where I enjoyed the speaker and knew right then that it might help me with what I thought I needed. I found that my attendance was transformative as I began to realize that I had choices in my life. Up until then, I had lived like someone who was hiding with no choices. The courses that were offered were designed to help one speak out and communicate. My wife took some EST courses too but she did not find that they suited her. I took the EST courses for 15 years, assisting the speakers and learning a little bit at a time.

"My wife and I were never on the same page; so after 37 years of marriage, I decided the kids didn't need me any longer and I needed to move on. One Sunday morning, out of the blue, I told my wife I was leaving. It just happened suddenly and took my wife by surprise. I grabbed my clothes and a couple of kitchen pots, which I threw into the backseat of my car, and I took off. I drove away for about 20 miles before what I had done really sank in! I felt such a sense of relief."

"*It took a substantial amount of courage for you to do that.*"

"Once I had left, there was no going back. My leaving really difficult for my wife. She did not understand why I left her after all our years together. I felt sorry for her, but it seemed as if she was still caught up in her childhood. She rated her father's and uncle's (the priest) opinions much higher than she did mine. Nothing I ever said to her seemed to register with her. It was as if we were two dead people, and I could not wake us up. Our marriage seemed like an obligation. I cared a lot about her because she was the mother of my children, but there was very little love between us. I know that in our marriage she was suffering too but I could no longer cope with all that negative energy. When I left, it was as if I rolled up a blanket that was suffocating me and my being was finally exposed to the light. In spite of our differences, I was able to stay friends with her at a distance.

"With the EST training, I was starting to look inward but I still could not talk about the war. I took their courses for 15 years but I was never able to talk about my war experience and my PTSD, the elephant in the room."

"Thankfully, you are able to share your story now. After your divorce, did you start dating?"

"I did start dating and over the years I had a number of relationships. I left my wife a couple of months before I moved to Vancouver again. My friend Guy LeFleur introduced me to a woman he knew. She came with him one night for dinner which I cooked. Oddly enough, I remember what I cooked. It was filet of Pacific cod with rice and vegetables. It's funny I can remember that dinner but I can't even remember what I cooked for dinner last night! She phoned me the next day, and we started going out. Just like that, we were in a relationship. She was employed as a nurse. I liked her well enough, but there were strange things about her. Naturally, she had a past life which I found out about, a little bit here and a little bit there. I soon learned she had a twin sister. Every time she didn't feel quite right about almost anything, she phoned her sister. So it seemed as if there were three of us in this relationship. I wondered if she had two personalities. It was as if after talking to her sister she was a different person. Before long, I moved to Victoria, and she followed me.

"Sometime later, I left and went to Calgary for three months. When I came back to my apartment in Victoria, she was there because she was hired to work in the hospital in Victoria. By then, our relationship wasn't working. Although there was something unstable about her, I had no idea what it was. Then, I found out she had been in psychiatric care so I moved her back to Vancouver where she could return to treatment. I remained living in Victoria where I bought an apartment building to renovate with another guy. I didn't have much money but I later I was able to buy him out.

"Somewhat later, I traveled to Montreal and then to Quebec City for the Merciers of America (my mother was a

Mercier) family reunion. There, I met a young woman who was a very distant relative of mine. After the reunion, she drove me to my motel, and we agreed to meet the next day. She was born in Sherbrooke, Quebec, and told me she had lived a very sheltered life. I gathered that was because she was still living with her parents. Her father was overly protective and kept a very close eye on his daughter. When I arrived at her house, he stood watching us from the front porch. It was also his habit to go with her to the skating rink and keep an eye on her so that she would not skate or hold hands with boys. By the time I met her, she had gotten over that!

"After the reunion, I returned to Victoria where I sold my apartment building and bought a nice house, overlooking the ocean. She joined me there but soon got tired of living in Victoria, so we moved to San Clemente, California, where I rented a penthouse on the ocean. Sometime later, we moved back to Canada, to Powell River where I bought a house and renovated it. To my regret, she could not adapt to living in Powell River where she had a job working with dementia patients. She fell for one of her coworkers and moved back to Montreal. I finished remodeling my house and moved to Montreal where I bought a house in Lachine, Quebec, and remodeled it. Perhaps, all this remodeling was a metaphor for me trying to rebuild my life.

We saw each other occasionally for a few years but we were very mismatched. One night, she decided to cook for me at her house. She was a pretty awful cook but she had taken a cooking course from a French chef in Montreal, so I thought it would be safe to go for dinner. That was a mistake! She put all of the pots on the stovetop, blasting on high to cook the food. I couldn't bear to watch her so I left and walked to the corner store for cigarettes. When I returned, we ate the main course which was terrible but she made a very nice dessert."

"What was it? Ice cream?"

"It was *Les Iles Flottantes* or 'Floating Islands.'

"While in Montreal, I decided to go to art school, which was a long held dream. At one time, when I was a child, I wanted to be an artist. I loved to draw. My parents did not think that was a useful activity and discouraged me from spending time creating art. Living in Montreal was one of the best times in my life.

"One day in the cafeteria on the campus of the art school I was attending, I could sense a young woman standing behind me in the line-up for food. She came over to the table where I had seated myself after I paid for my food and asked if she could join me. At the time, I could pass for 45, but she was only 26. Nevertheless, we started chatting, and I found out she was finishing an advanced degree in languages and would soon become a translator. She called me four days later. She began inviting me to the theatre, opera, and symphonies which I had never done before but thoroughly enjoyed. Before long, we developed a very pleasant relationship in which I believe I became a father figure to her. Her own father had abused her. She seemed somewhat fearful but she was also frank and down-to-earth.

"When I moved back to British Columbia, we remained friends and chatted occasionally on the phone. She has come a few times to visit me in Sechelt where I live now. The last time she visited, we were chatting in my living room when she jumped up and started taking off her clothes! That disrobing was meant to make her feel free and open, nothing more. At that moment, the doorbell rang, and she ran to answer it and opened the door! I was left wondering what my neighbors thought. Although I met many wonderful and interesting women through the years, none of my relationships with them worked out for any length of time.

"Having a woman love me scared me, and I tended to push her away. A number of them had their own emotional problems that interfered with our relationships. I chose women who were remarkably beautiful but who unfortunately attracted the attention of other men. Now, after living alone for 37 years, it's hard to find another person who is compatible. Over the years, I have learned to cope with living my by myself and I now find I am content with my life. I do not want the agony and pain of another relationship."

Chapter 23

'You gain strength, courage and confidence
by every experience in which you really stop to look fear in
the face. You are able to say to yourself, 'I lived through this
horror. I can take the next thing that comes along.''
– Eleanor Roosevelt

"What I find compelling about your story is that although you've had a life full of challenges and adversity, you have not wallowed in self-pity. You have treated your difficulties as learning experiences and you have used them to create a better life for yourself. As a result of your attitude and hard work, you have become a stronger and more balanced person. Would you agree?"

"Well, I am working on it. I believe that situations and relationships are thrown at us for a purpose and it is up to us to figure out what we need to learn from them. And time gives you a different perspective. I've never thought of myself as a hero though. I just did what I was supposed to do, which was to survive. Years after the war, I made pilgrimages to Germany where I meditated with Germans and others who were also members of the spiritual group I belong to.

"My birth parents did not bring me home to join the family until I was 14 months old and even then they did not spend much time with me. I think they were very busy working hard to cope with their large family and keep the farm running. The result was that I had very little time alone with them, and we did not bond as we might have if I had been with them from birth. It was not known at the time how important it is for both parents to spend the time to bond with their baby.

"My mother was a very devout Roman Catholic. There were retreats for Catholic women that my mother attended where they were indoctrinated as to how they should behave. Her threat to us when we misbehaved was that she would tell *le Curé*, the local priest who was held in the highest esteem. One never ignored his proclamations. The priest craft controlled every facet of our lives including everything from birth control to rearing children. My mother was very strong and worked so hard looking after the family that she had very little time to pursue her own interests. At times, she talked a lot and had a very loud voice. That was in contrast to her sweet singing voice with which she sang lullabies to her babies to get them to sleep. Only at bedtime did she sing. However, when she stood on the back porch and called us home for dinner or any other reason, the neighbors who lived a mile away could hear her!

"At the time, I didn't fully understand my parents' lack of response to my service during the war but years later I realized how proud they were of me (or at least my mother, who I knew loved me). My parents' home burned down in 1957. They managed to get their piano out of the house, down the stairs, and into the yard with the picture of the King and me standing up on top. It never fell off. (Perhaps, it was glued to the surface of the piano!) My Dad lost all faith in banks after living through Great Depression. He hid money in canning jars which he then buried in the basement floor under the stairs that lead to the lower level. After the fire, he returned to the house and dug up the containers of money. Good thing he didn't hide his money under his mattress!

"My father was a difficult man. He did not usually talk much to anyone. But to me, he rarely said a word except to tell me I was no good. Under those circumstances, it was difficult to ever feel self-confident. I moved to Bonnyville to be near him during his last months of life. One evening, three months before his death, I was visiting with him in the hospital. We decided to go out in the car for a change of scenery. I helped move him into a wheelchair, and we went outside. While I pushed the wheelchair along the sidewalk toward the car, it hit a bump I did not see in the dark. I came very close to dumping him into a snowbank. That unleashed some very unkind words from him. Even on his deathbed where I sat for days beside him, he never acknowledged me except to say I would never be any good. I had hoped he would say to me just once that he loved me, but he never did. It would have been so nice. However, at least now I have some understanding of why he may have behaved the way he did. It seems to me he repeated the mess he grew up in, having had no role model on how to parent a child. Also, I realize how much pressure he was under to keep his family fed and clothed plus his business of farming functioning well during very challenging economic times."

"It seems your father was a good example of how not to raise children. It is very unfortunate your father didn't have a relationship with you. He missed out on an opportunity to get to know you."

"During the time period in which I was growing up, I don't think parents were aware of how their children were affected by their parenting style. I never felt I was loved by my family. My father set a poor example for me to follow for child rearing. I wasn't a very good father and I made a lot of mistakes with my children. I don't like to think about it because I know I have hurt them. I didn't know how to love or be loved. I was never able to make anyone else happy because I couldn't make myself happy."

"Was there anyone in your life who you felt was a role model for you when you were growing up?"

"There was my Aunt Aurora who was married to my father's older brother. She was the one who took care of me when I was a baby. Later, when she came to visit, she would always cuddle me and call me terms of endearment. I always felt a strong connection with her but did not know why until many years later.

"I was a brother to six sisters. My three older sisters all became nuns. One day, two very large touring cars showed up on our doorstep. The priest and nuns in the cars were on a recruitment mission from a convent in California. My oldest sister who had been in a convent since she was six years old left with them and two other sisters followed later. There were probably several reasons why they left Bonnyville for California. I think the girls were quite devout, and my mother wanted them to get an education and not have a life like hers. It was also quite a feather in my parents' cap to have so many children join an order of nuns. Many years later, two of my sisters returned to Canada. They bought a house in Calgary and began teaching careers. My other sister remained in California where she just recently celebrated her 100th birthday and 80 years as a nun. They were all likely quite disappointed when I resisted joining the priest craft.

"My youngest sister and I are the most alike of any of the siblings in our family. She is 15 years younger than I am, but the differences in our ages have never been an obstacle. We have the same sense of humor and can effortlessly connect with each other. We also share the same sense of spirituality.

"In later years, the siblings who tormented me as a child reconciled with me regarding their behavior. Naturally, this greatly improved our relationship. It meant a lot to me that they recognized what they had done to me and how difficult my life was as a result. My brother who caused me the most grief was kicked in the face by one of our horses when he was a young child. I think the resulting facial deformity caused him to feel inadequate. His feelings of inferiority fueled his tormenting of me. Who knows, though, if I had a happier life as a child, perhaps, I would not have enlisted in the military but stayed at home and become a farmer like them. I would have missed a valuable part of my life.

"It was devastating to have a father and some siblings who didn't seem to love me. In spite of that feeling of being dropped into the wrong family, I did learn some very valuable skills on the farm that I believe saved my life during the war. Struggling to find my place in the world also allowed me to learn to persevere, to accept and be accepted, and to work hard to accomplish my dreams. Besides, nothing is ever black and white or good and bad.

"When I returned from the war, I was really struggling with PTSD and adjustment to civilian life. My wife and I really didn't know each other well enough to make a commitment like marriage but we rushed into it anyway. I wanted to go to California with her to visit my sisters and she would only go if we were married. We were not in love with each other. In fact, my wife was in love with someone else at the time. The war had a profound effect on me and although the war was over, there was a war going on inside of me. As would be expected, that emotional turmoil spilled over into to my everyday life and my marriage. My wife and I were never in harmony with each other and could not communicate in any meaningful way. As soon as I walked in the door from work, she complained and criticized me which I think stemmed from her own unhappiness. Her uncle who was a priest and her father had far more influence in her life than I did. It was not that she was a bad person because she had many good qualities. She was very unhappy, and I could not make her love me. I did not love myself so how could I genuinely love anyone else? We gradually slipped into the habit of drinking alcohol which continued for many years until I was drinking a bottle of scotch every evening.

"In spite of our marriage difficulties, my wife was a very good mother, and I am grateful for our five children. I had such a struggle finding my way to satisfactory employment in the early years after the war that I did not want my sons to experience the problems I encountered. I decided to create a business that might interest them. They did not want to go to university but they liked carpentry and building things so that's the path we took. The downside of my plan was that my working long hours had a detrimental effect on my younger children while they were growing up. I was not able to spend as much time with them as I would have liked. This was particularly true of my fourth son and my daughter, our youngest child. We were not close because I did not make time for them. I feel really badly that I let them down. At the time, I was pretty injured myself and I think having felt unloved as a child meant I did not have a road map on how to love my children. I did not give my daughter the attention she deserved. I thought it was my wife's job to care of her and that hurt my daughter.

"I have apologized to my children for my absence and inattention but nothing can make up for those lost years. Although in my heart, I loved my kids but I did not show my love through my actions. I did not know how. In spite of what I think was poor parenting, my intentions were good and although my 'piano might have had some false cords,' my children have all turned out well. Each one is successful in his/her own right and each with their individual characteristics have become persons I am very proud of. My youngest son lives on Vancouver Island where he worked as an arborist and now has a consulting business. My daughter has a family and lives on a ranch in Alberta. My two middle sons are still in the construction building homes in the town where I now live. My oldest son is in charge of the truss factory we built in Alberta.

"I knew nothing about unconditional love and I did not know what my kids needed. However, I can see that my grandchildren are raising their children in a whole different way. I love to see the obvious love and joy in their relationships. I am lucky enough to have 35 descendants, 22 of whom are great grandchildren. I am learning every day that love is the most wonderful gift in life. I am now able to tell my children that I love them. It has been a long road to get this point in my life but it was well worth the journey.

Marcel's Family in the Seventies
Back left to right: Guy, Berthe, Marcel, George, Brian
Front: Edouard and Joanne

Chapter 24

'That is the way it was. This is the way it is.'
– Marcel Croteau

"Marcel, you have told me that the spirituality that you have embraced has greatly affected your life and recovery from trauma. How would you describe your state of grace?"

"The greatest fault of humanity is its separateness. It fractures unity, it creates countries, it starts wars. It has been that way for an eternity. I have embraced what for me is a new way of thinking which has helped me to see the way things are and the way they could be and that brings everything into focus for me. It is as if the whole universe and consciousness are all one. There's no separateness and only man and his kind make separateness. When that concept is accepted by everyone on the planet and lives in the minds of humanity, it will be the end of wars and the end of suffering. Many historical figures have recognized the energy that is there to create this harmony. It's interesting to me because this idea takes us beyond our separateness, out of our little corners of the world and shows us the whole picture. It's not a belief, it's about knowing and experiencing it. As if I know that I know that I know. It's not about my church is better than your church. It's not about that. It's an open thing, wide open. When people want to join, it's completely voluntary with no pressure, expectations, or requirements. It is not that I am against organized religion but it just no longer works for me. I do appreciate, though, being able occasionally to go to a place where people pray. The energy there is very calming. That's where I'm at.

"Since I joined this meditation group in 2001 it has taken me from what I have described earlier, such as the old thought patterns and feelings, to have a better understanding of myself and the world around me. I have become who I now am spiritually and emotionally through meditation and attending several retreats in New Zealand and Germany. The last one I went to was the most profound. I have learned that through meditation you become one with everything. We are all one consciousness. Meditation takes one beyond the smallness that we are to the realization that everything from living creatures to inanimate objects to the landscape around us is a collection of atoms vibrating at different rates. This activity creates a universal consciousness. When you achieve the consciousness that we are all one, it changes your outlook on your life. Dangerous radicals think that they're going to change the world by killing people to gain attention to their cause. I saw enough killings in World War II and believe me that changed me forever. It kicked a part of my humanity out of me. How little I knew when I joined the Air Force. I had been raised on the farm during the Depression in a strict Catholic family. The consciousness was very small, but it was not because they were bad people. It was a lack of knowledge and inexperience in the world. No one looked beyond their small world. The priest craft made sure that people stayed there in that mindset so that they could control their parishioners. It was a mental prison that was created by the church. That's what it was all about, controlling people through fear. That is why I left the church.

It took me more than 20 years to ease off that belief system before growing into a much broader perspective.

"My youngest sister has been with this meditation group for 35 years and introduced me to it. I start my day with meditation which allows me to become part of one consciousness. This brings in the light which is God. I send out the light to my family and then to the whole country and then to each continent and so forth. I've had experiences where the light is just raining around me. I remember when I was young I saw a picture in the Bible of light coming down from the sky and that's what it's like. We are all connected in the light. All of that is an important part of my life. I recently went to see my doctor who told me I am healthy, my only issue is an ingrown toenail. He asked me what my secret was. I said 'it's what I think and what I eat.' The doctor said he couldn't argue with that. I believe we are what our thought forms are and we become that. You know the Hebrew saying 'as you sow, so shall you reap.'"

"I wonder how long it will take before the world becomes a better place through this knowledge of consciousness?"

"I think time is irrelevant. What is time anyway? However, I believe we will change, but we have to be patient. It can begin with one person. You have to work within your own circle. It is similar to when you take a bunch of pebbles and throw them into a pool of water. All the rings of water around each pebble overlap each other with the energy combining and continuing to spread. Our consciousness is like that. Every atom in the world sends out its energy like the pebbles so the energy of every atom in the world knows all their energies overlap and become combined, acting as one. It's part of creation that there is an infinite variety of combinations of atoms. That is what makes our world the way it is. We are so small individually, which is one of the realities. However, we have the capability to become one if we so choose. This is our truth and this truth is also reality.

"Joining this meditation group was not like getting hit over the head with a doctrine like you do with some religions. There are no sinners. Although to me it seemed that the church I grew up in was very dogmatic and restrictive, I have found that the Roman Catholic Church has changed since then. It has become more modern and is not the same as it was when I was a kid growing up. When I got married, it was my wife's uncle who was the priest for our wedding. He told us to be like the little birds and just breed once a year! He had been in our community for 27 years and was the one who baptized me. He wore pince-nez glasses and he looked down on everyone, figuratively and literally. When I think of what we were told and how we were controlled by the local priest when I was a child, I shudder. Recently, I went to my brother's funeral in Alberta at my old church. The priest was Filipino and he was funny and engaging but he also exhibited a seriousness and an openness I had not previously experienced in the church. I had not been to a Catholic service for a long time, so it was refreshing to see how much it has changed."

"What attracted you to your sister's and her husband's form of spirituality?"

"My life was really difficult during the years when I was married to someone with whom I could not connect and when the effects of PTSD were quite severe. By 2001, I had done a lot of work on myself through the EST training. I came out of it realizing that I had choices. However, although I had studied diligently to improve myself, I was not totally satisfied with my progress. I definitely was not the person I am now. But I had begun the process to look at myself and I realized that the war was finished in 1945, but there was still a war going on within me. My participation in the war had affected my very existence. I questioned what we had been doing to be involved in a war, no matter what our best intentions were. Many other questions haunted me too. Eventually, I responded to my sister's encouragement and made the decision to join her meditation group. Gradually, I began to realize that there was something to be learned from every experience we have in life. I needed to be able to look for some knowledge or insight, then move on and not get stuck. Also, I learned it is necessary to be flexible and to allow change to happen. It is the only way to emerge healed from the effects of our struggles with our life experiences. I believe I have been able to accomplish that through study and meditation and the realization that there is this consciousness and interconnection among all of us. That is not to say I have all the answers or completed the journey but at least I am fortunate to have lived long enough to say I am making progress."

"Well, it's not how long you live but how you live your life. You've had a long remarkable life but you have also lived it well and have gained a great deal of insight from your experiences which thankfully you are willing to share."

"It is easy for me to express myself if I have someone who is interested in what I have to say. I really enjoy my conversations with you where I can express myself. Even as we talk, I am understanding more about myself. It took me a long time to learn that my struggle was all here, within me. Instead, for a long time, I fought my battles out there."

"It seems to me that most people are afraid to look inward in order to examine themselves but clearly you are not afraid of doing that."

"But I was carefully guarding my inner struggles the whole time I took those 15 years of EST courses. I never told any of those I met that I had been in the war. I hid everything. I was really blocked and fearful."

"Thankfully, you are now able to talk about your war experiences and a lot of other life events. And to share your insights."

"Now, I feel I am surrounded by the light and I am still every day discovering who I am and how I should live this life. It's like peeling off the layers of an onion except that it is a task you never finish. I ask myself why I didn't start this process long ago. I should have asked questions much sooner but I feel lucky to have been able to study and transform how I think and how I look at the world and how I receive it. Now, I perceive that the whole universe is around me and within me and we are all one."

"That explains why I weigh as much as I do. I have the whole universe within me and it is weighing very heavily on me! I am being silly of course because I do find the whole concept of what you are saying to be very compelling. I love listening to our recorded conversations when I am transcribing them because they are full of so much laughter."

"There has always been a part of me that has wanted to be joyful. Early on, I discovered the healing nature of laughter. I always wanted to be funny but it did not always happen as I intended. Humor was not a valued attribute in my strict Roman Catholic upbringing. I know there is more than one way to find one's spirituality. It's just a question of finding a form that works for you. It is not in the church or in a building. It is in the minerals, trees, plants, the water, and the oceans. It's the oneness of creation. It's the light. Everything depends on the light."

"So you're attributing this knowledge of the light to finding well-being."

"Yes. I've worked on myself every day for 37 years and each day I am discovering new things about who I am and how I should live my life. I've seen many changes in the span of my long life. From horse and buggy and no electricity to mechanization, space exploration, computers, and the digital age…and now vehicles that can drive themselves! And I too have undergone tremendous change in many ways. I am no longer that frightened child who was afraid to speak for himself. I have managed to send my PTSD to a place within me where it no longer rules my life. There are many things I can no longer do (including indulging in my favorite drink which was Courvoisier with a drop or two of maple syrup). However, I feel blessed that I've had this much time in my life to discover more about myself and to live my life as I want. I am happy that at age 78 I discovered that I have a tenor singing voice. At age 72, I was finally able to go to art school, a long-held dream. I feel privileged to have been able to do that. Many never have the opportunity to discover their own creativity. I have friends and family around me who add joy and meaning to my life. Also, it seems too that I am a bit of a storyteller which I have come to realize since starting this project.

"Above all, I have found a spirituality that has enabled me to learn a way of thinking that has offered me knowledge and understanding of myself and the world around me. Everything is about love and beauty but as humans, we make life dark and it becomes a struggle to disengage ourselves from those thought patterns. However, to be happy I think each person has to find his own way. One needs to be open to change. For me, it was like climbing a steep set of stairs but I figured out how to take one step at a time. I have not yet reached the top of that 'mountain' but I have escaped my prison because I have found a knowledge that is right for me.

"Our life experiences, good or bad, shape who we are. My life as a young boy, as a war veteran, as a husband, as a father, and as a friend still exists in me and remains a part of who I was and in many ways has allowed me to become the person I want to be. For that, I am grateful. I've lived a long life and I am not afraid to die because once you accept your mortality it allows you to live one day at a time in the best way possible. It is as if I do not have a strong resistance to death now that I've accepted that it is reality. I am at peace.

"So that is the way it is."

Marcel's Paintings

Marcel's Interpretation of Monet's Le Pont d'Arignon

Portrait from Art School